AF750527

CHESTERFIELD CENTRAL LIBRARY

REFERENCE LIBRARY

Class No. 346

Acc. No.

DERBYSHIRE LIBRARY SERV

WITHDRAW

DATE

BUTTERWORTHS
ANNOTATED LEGISLATION
SERVICE

STATUTES SUPPLEMENT No. 218

THE LOCAL GOVERNMENT ACT 1974

By

DAVID FOULKES, LL.M., J.P.,

Barrister; Senior Lecturer in Law, University of Wales
Institute of Science and Technology, Cardiff;
Member, South Glamorgan County Council

LONDON
BUTTERWORTHS
1974

CHESTERFIELD PUBLIC LIBRARIES

CLASS NO.	346		
ACC. NO.			
Vendor	Date	P.P.	N.P.
S.O.	10/74	–	–
Lab'l'd	Pr'c's'd	Cat'd	Checked
		✓	
REBOUND			

ENGLAND: BUTTERWORTH & CO. (PUBLISHERS) LTD.
LONDON: 88 KINGSWAY, WC2B 6AB

AUSTRALIA: BUTTERWORTHS PTY. LTD.
SYDNEY: 586 PACIFIC HIGHWAY, CHATSWOOD, NSW 2067
MELBOURNE: 343 LITTLE COLLINS STREET, 3000
BRISBANE: 240 QUEEN STREET, 4000

CANADA: BUTTERWORTH & CO. (CANADA) LTD.
TORONTO: 2265 MIDLAND AVENUE,
SCARBOROUGH M1P 4S1

NEW ZEALAND: BUTTERWORTHS OF NEW ZEALAND LTD.
WELLINGTON: 26–28 WARING TAYLOR STREET, 1

SOUTH AFRICA: BUTTERWORTH & CO. (SOUTH AFRICA) (PTY.) LTD.
DURBAN: 152–154 GALE STREET

Chesterfield

©
BUTTERWORTH & CO. (PUBLISHERS) LTD.
1974

ISBN: 0 406 54730 0

PRINTED IN GREAT BRITAIN BY OFFSET LITHOGRAPHY BY
BILLING AND SONS LTD., GUILDFORD AND LONDON

PREFACE

This book seeks to explain the provisions of the Local Government Act 1974, which received the Royal Assent on 8th February 1974. The Act is divided into four Parts relating respectively to grants, rating, local government administration and miscellaneous matters, and the arrangement of the book follows that of the Act.

Part I of the Act, which is dealt with in Chapter 1, *post*, established a new system of grants for local authorities and in particular introduces a new rate support grant system as from 1st April 1974.

Part II of the Act, which is dealt with in Chapter 2, *post*, makes changes in rating law. It introduces a new rate rebate scheme, amends the law relating to the rating of unoccupied property, imposes a compulsory surcharge on unused commercial property, extends the exemption for facilities for disabled persons and provides that valuation lists are not to be altered on account of central heating installations or minor structural alterations.

Part III introduces an entirely new dimension in local government administration by creating an "Ombudsman" system for local government parallel to that already established for central government. The new machinery will enable individuals or bodies of persons who have suffered injustice in consequence of local government maladministration to complain to members of the Commissions for Local Administration which are established for England and Wales. In Chapter 3, *post*, I have dealt with the new complaints procedure at some length, particularly as an understanding of the system requires some knowledge of the work of the Parliamentary Commissioner.

Part IV of the Act, which contains miscellaneous and general matters, is dealt with in Chapter 4.

The Act itself, with annotations, follow after Chapter 4. Each section of the Act is followed by an "Explanatory Note". This gives the reference to the numbered paragraphs of Chapters 1 to 4 in which the section is explained.

May 1974 DAVID FOULKES

CONTENTS

INTRODUCTION

The Local Government Act 1974 received the Royal Assent on 8th February 1974. It was one of the few Bills rescued from the legislative holocaust brought about by the dissolution of Parliament on that date.

The Act is in four Parts. The first provides a new rate support grant system as from 1st April 1974. It was for this reason that it was essential for the Bill to be enacted before the dissolution, as the orders and regulations providing for the fixing and paying of the grant could not be made until enactment. The late introduction of the Bill into Parliament—at the end of October 1973—had been criticized as leaving little enough time for discussion. As things turned out, the only stage taken in the Lords was the second reading. None of the many amendments put down for the Committee stage—some by the Government itself—could be considered.

The second Part of the Act makes changes in rating law. The third Part provides for an Ombudsman system in local government, and the fourth contains miscellanea.

The Act was described by the Government as a necessary adjunct to the 1974 reorganisation. It does not pretend to deal in a major way with local government finance, and opposition amendments to provide new sources of local authority revenue were resisted.

The Act came into force on 8th February 1974, except for Part II, sections 35, 37 and 42, and Schedules 6, 7 and 8. For the dates of commencement of those provisions see the note to s. 43 of the Act, p. 80, *post*.

The Act does not extend to Scotland or Northern Ireland except in so far as it amends the House of Commons Disqualification Act 1957 by providing that members of the new Commissions for Local Administration are disqualified from membership of the House of Commons and the Northern Ireland Assembly.

CHAPTER ONE
GRANTS

RATE SUPPORT GRANT

CALCULATION OF RATE SUPPORT GRANT

[1] The concept of the rate support grant was introduced by the Local Government Act 1966. The formula for calculating it under that Act had become, it was generally agreed, outdated. The 1974 Act therefore provides a new formula for the year 1974–5 and each subsequent year.

[2] The grant is calculated as follows.[1] The Secretary of State determines *the amount available for grants*, that is, the amount available for the payment of grants to local authorities in respect of their *relevant expenditure* for the year in question. Relevant expenditure means the expenditure falling to be defrayed out of the rate fund, reduced by the amount of certain payments made into the rate fund (s. 1 (4) (*a*)) and excluding certain specified items. The latter include sums paid to another authority by virtue of a precept, and the payment of mandatory student awards and grants for teacher-training students (s. 1 (5)). (Specific central government grants of 90 per cent. are provided for such awards and grants.)

[3] In arriving at *the amount available for grants* account is not taken of housing subsidies and certain specific grants paid to rating authorities in respect of rate and rebate schemes and to local education authorities in respect of the awards and grants referred to in the previous paragraph.

[4] From *the amount available for grants* thus ascertained is deducted a portion of that amount representing grants for certain specific services, for national parks and for transport supplementary grants. The amount available after making those deductions is *the estimated aggregate amount of the rate support grants* for that year.

[5] Before determining the amount available for grants, and the portion to be deducted from it in respect of the grants referred to in the preceding paragraph, the Secretary of State is required to consult with local authority associations etc. He is also required to take into account certain factors, some of which are in the same terms as in the 1966 Act, *e.g.*, the fluctuation in the demand for and the need to develop services. The wording relating to price levels etc. is however significantly different (s. 1 (3)).

[6] The *estimated aggregate amount of the rate support grants* is fixed by a rate support grant order made by the Secretary of State with the consent of the Treasury. It is in force for one year for 12 months from 1st April.[2] Under the

[1] S. 1.

[2] For 1974–5, see S.I. 1974 No. 550 and No. 428.

1966 Act an order was in force for two years. An order has to be laid before the Commons, and does not have effect until approval by a resolution of that House. With the order has to to be laid a report of the considerations leading to the provisions of the order (s. 3). (For 1974–5 order see H.C. 33 of 1974.)

ELEMENTS OF RATE SUPPORT GRANT

[7] As under the 1966 Act, the Secretary of State is required to divide the aggregate amount of the rate support grants into three elements, the needs element, the domestic element and the resources element, and to prescribe in the rate support grant order the aggregate amounts of the first two elements named, and the estimated aggregate amount of the resources element (s. 2).

The needs element

How it is calculated

[8] The 1966 formula of basic payment, specified supplementary payments, specified provision for Inner London, etc. is abandoned. The 1974 Act provides[3] that the needs element payable to local authorities is to be the aggregate of (a) an amount arrived at by multiplying a prescribed sum by the population of the area and (b) additional amounts determined in the way prescribed in the rate support grants order and attributed to such *additional factors* as may be prescribed. Population is therefore the only factor required by statute to be taken into account. This is because it is the basic determinant of expenditure. All other factors are as prescribed in the order. This is designed to give the greatest possible flexibility. The *additional factors* are referred to below.

[9] The needs element thus arrived at is adjusted by reference to expenditure in connection with certain pooled educational facilities and may be further adjusted by reference to expenditure on research into and training in local authority facilities, on education for persons suffering from disability, etc. Regulations may be made for ascertaining the amount by which the needs element is to be adjusted for these reasons. Any difference between the estimated and actual amounts involved is to be adjusted in a subsequent payment of the needs element.

[10] The *additional factors* in the 1974–75 order are:

(i) the number of "education units" (determined by reference to the number of primary and nursery school pupils, secondary and special and direct grant school pupils non-advanced further education students, and school meals provided).

(ii) personal social service units. This is a new factor which takes into account the number of children in care, social work staff, home help, day care places, meals served at home, clubs and centres, persons in residential accommodation, and persons over 65.

(iii) population decline over the decade 1962–1972. The justification given for this is that the same services are being supplied to a reduced population. Local authorities accepted, to the Ministers' surprise, that an

[3] Sch. 2, Part I.

increase in population did not require to be treated as a separate factor: it would, it was thought, be adequately reflected through the other factors in the needs element.

(iv) acreage in excess of 1·5 per head.

Additional weightings are given to inner South-East, outer South-East and certain West Midlands counties, and the total given by the formula is increased by 3 per cent. for each London Borough.

[**11**] An amendment was moved at the Committee stage of the Bill to provide an extra sum for metropolitan areas. The Minister, while recognizing that in the past conurbations had not received their proper share of the grant, resisted the amendment on the ground that in introducing an obligatory element into the grant, it would reduce the complete flexibility that was desired. As we have seen, in 1974–5 there is a special weighting for certain metropolitan areas. In future years the problems of those areas might be more appropriately dealt with by a variation of the resources element.

To whom it is paid

[**12**] Subject to what is said below, the needs element is payable to all councils, except those of a non-metropolitan district.[4]

(i) The Bill originally provided that the needs element would not be payable to a non-metropolitan district council. The reason given was that the non-metropolitan county would account for 80 to 90 per cent. of local government spending in its area chiefly because of its education and highway functions. An amendment was proposed in Committee which would enable the Minister to ensure payment of the needs element to such a council. In support it was argued that if no needs element was payable to such a council, the rates levied by the rating authority for district purposes would appear artificially high, and the county precept artificially low. The amendment would also, it was said, give an added degree of flexibility. The government agreed to alter the regulations governing the make-up of the rate demand note to make the position clearer to ratepayers and the amendment was withdrawn. See S.I. 1974 No. 363.

But the government moved an amendment at the Report stage which now appears as s. 2 (4) of the Act. This does give the Minister power to provide in regulations for a proportion of the needs element payable to a non-metropolitan county to be payable instead to the councils of districts in the county. Different provisions may be made in relation to different councils. The government disclaimed however, any intention of making any such regulations at present.

(ii) The Secretary of State can by regulations provide that part of the needs element payable to a London borough council or to a metropolitan district council shall instead be payable to the Greater London Council or, as the case may be, to the metropolitan county council (s. 2 (3)).

The domestic element

[**13**] This was introduced by the 1966 Act. It was designed to protect the domestic ratepayer from the burden of rates on his dwelling. Under that Act a

---

[4] S. 2 (3), (4), (5).

uniform amount was prescribed in the rate support grant order to be deducted from what would otherwise be the rate poundage falling on residential property. The 1974 Act provides for a variable rate relief system—"different amounts in the pound may be prescribed for different rating areas".[5] The Minister explained, "We intend to use this to give most relief in the areas which will be receiving a smaller share of grant next year [1974–5] and where reorganisation will lead to a sharp increase in the water and sewerage charges". The Conservative government had intended fixing a minimum domestic element of 7p, increased in some areas to as much as 40p. However, the Labour government decided that the domestic element should be 13p throughout England and 33·5p throughout Wales.

The resources element

[14] Under the 1966 formula the resources element was paid only where the amount per head of an authority's population which a penny rate produced was less than the national average per head. The resources element could be used only to bring an authority's resources up to the national average. It was recognised that this did not provide sufficient resources element in those areas which needed extra supprt.

[15] Under the new formula[6] payment can be made to an authority where the *rateable value per head* of that authority's population is less than the *national standard rateable value per head* of the population. The former is defined in the Act, and the latter is "of such amount as may be prescribed" in the rate support grant order. This gives a greater flexibility. It has been fixed for 1974–5 at £154.

How is the resources element calculated?

[16] The *local deficiency in rateable value* has first to be calculated. This is the product of: (a) the difference between rateable value per head and the national standard rateable value; and (b) the area's population.

This *local deficiency* is then multiplied by the *uniform rate* for the area. The Bill originally provided that it was to be multiplied by the general rate, but an amendment was moved at the Report stage to take account of those cases where different rates are levied in different parts of an authority's area—hence the *uniform rate*. The Minister said, "The number and importance of the amounts levied in parts only of a rating area will be greatly increased as a result of an order which will be laid before the House shortly dealing with differential rating. . . . The scheme for differential rating will phase the elimination of these differentials over a period of five years. During that period it is necessary to have this power to calculate the uniform rate."[7]

[17] Para. 11 of Schedule 2, also introduced by amendment at the Report stage, deals with the situation that arises where valuations are reduced retrospectively, and the effect is to reduce, by an amount greater than that specified by the Secretary of State, the aggregate of the *effective rateable values* of all

[5] Sch. 2, para. 5 (1).
[6] Sch. 2, Part III.
[7] See s. 1.

hereditaments in the authority's area. In such circumstances the resources element will be recalculated to take this into account. Note that the authority must ask the Secretary of State to act in this matter.[8]

[18] The resources element is not payable to a county council or the G.L.C. —*i.e.*, it is payable to rating authorities. As originally drafted the Bill would in certain circumstances have deprived metropolitan district councils and London boroughs of the resource element. The intention was to withold this element from a poor district in an generally rich county. Local authority associations objected to this. The Minister said that the power was unlikely to be used and the provision was dropped from the Bill.

VARIATION OF RATE SUPPORT GRANT ORDERS

[19] Section 4 permits, as did the 1966 Act, the variation by the Secretary of State of a rate support grant order. The matters which may be taken into account in making a variation order differ in some respects from those listed in the 1966 Act. The position now is that if it appears to the Secretary of State that after determining the *amount available for grants* the *relevant expenditure* of local authorities has been or is likely to be substantially increased by certain matters (see below) he may redetermine that amount, and may by order increase the amounts fixed by the rate support grant order for the year as the *estimated aggregate amount of the rate support grants* and the aggregate amount of the needs element for that year. (Such order will specify the actual and not the estimated aggregate amount of the resources element for that year. The reason for this is that the resources element, being calculated on the basis of the actual rate poundage, cannot be known at the time the rate support grant order is made, but is known at the time of a variation order.)

[20] The "certain matters" referred to above are (a) an increase which has taken place in the level of prices, costs or remuneration, or (b) the coming into operation of a provision of an enactment passed after this Act ((b) is new). In redetermining the amount available for grants by reason of those matters, the Minister must take into account not only the effect of the increase referred to in (a) or of the provision referred to in (b), but also any future variation in the level of prices which will result from "final decisions". An example is where a pay rise has been agreed, but will not come into effect for some time. Apart from a change resulting from the coming into operation of an enactment ((b) above), the Minister can not take account of any change, since the first determination of the amount available for grants, in the demand for or need to develop services.

[21] Section 4 (5) was added at the Report stage. The Minister's explanation can be paraphrased thus.[9] When a rate support grant order is made, a certain ratio between needs and resources element is assumed. The latter element is distributed in ignorance of the actual rate poundage and rate poundages may be set at such a level that most of increase in the amount available for grants (by way of a variation order) would be preempted by authorities' resources elements entitlements, leaving little or nothing to be added to the needs element.

[8] Sch. 2, para. 11 (1) (*c*).
[9] 867 H. of C. Official Report 1685.

If, in the Secretary of State's view, the ratio between the two elements would for this reason be significantly different from the assumed or *expected ratio*, he would be able to specify in the variation order an aggregate amount of the resources element which he judged would bear the *expected ratio*, he would be able to specify in the variation order an aggregate amount of the rescources element which he judged would bear the *expected ratio* to the needs element—*i.e.*, he could adjust the figures of the two elements to bring them back into line. In addition the Secretary of State would by the order alter such authority's entitlement to the resources element.

REDUCTION OF GRANT IN CASE OF DEFAULT

[**22**] By s. 5 (1), if the Minister (a) is satisfied that an authority has failed to achieve or maintain a reasonable standard in the discharge of any of its functions, and (b) thinks that a reduction should therefore be made in the amounts of any elements of rate support grant he may lay a report before Parliament stating the reasons for and the amount of proposed reductions.[10] If the report is approved by the Commons the Secretary of State may then carry out the proposed reductions. The authority must be given a hearing.

[**23**] By s. 5 (2) the Minister may make regulations for prescribing "standards and general requirements in relation to any function of a local authority". In deciding whether an authority has failed to come up to the standard required by s. 5 (1) regard shall be had to such regulations and any other standards or requirements imposed under any enactment. There is no need to comment here on the significance of this power for central—local government relations.

[**24**] At the Report stage an amendment was moved which would have permitted the Minister to reduce the grant on another ground, namely, if he thought the authority had too many staff. The Minister, whilst stating that there was some public unease in the matter, was unable to accept the amendment, on two grounds, first that the basis of the 1974 reorganisation is that local authorities should be more not less independent, and second, that central government was not capable of doing the job involved.

[**25**] This section of the Bill originally contained a subsection applying s. 99 (1) of the Education Act to any failure to discharge a duty imposed by the regulations referred to above but after discussion in Committee it was withdrawn.[11]

TRANSPORT SUPPLEMENTARY GRANT

[**26**] Section 6 provides for a new system of transport grants, operative as from 1st April 1975. The system was explained in Department of the Environment circulars 104/73 and 27/74. The grants are payable to county councils and the G.L.C. in respect of estimated expense in connection with *transport matters*. These are defined as, public transport, highways, the regulation of traffic and

[10] This section of the Act follows the Local Government Act 1966, s. 4, which in turn followed the Local Government Act 1958, s. 3—hence the reference to those sections in s. 5 (3) of this Act.

[11] The deleted subsection was previously s. 4 (4) of the Local Government Act 1966. For Committee discussion, see H. of C. Official Report, S.C.A., 27th November 1973, cols. 109–112.

the provision of parking places. Included are therefore, expenditure on the construction, improvement and maintenance of highways, signposting, lighting, pedestrianisation measures, road safety education and training, landscaping and other environmental measures, the provision of cycle-tracks, lorry parks, off-street parking, etc.

[**27**] One particular point raised in committee was whether expenditure on providing facilities in connection with the loading or unloading of freight could qualify for grant. The result is s. 6 (2), introduced at the Report stage. Note the reference there to capital expenditure. Apart from this the new grant does not distinguish between capital and current expenditure.

[**28**] The total amount of grant is fixed in the rate support grant order. The amount payable to a council is the amount by which its "accepted" estimated transport expenditure (that is, as accepted by the Secretary of State) exceeds the amount determined by the Secretary of State as appropriate to be taken into account for this purpose. In determining this he must "have regard to the progress which appears to him to have been made by the council in formulating and implementing suitable [transport] policies . . ." (s. 6 (5)). Each council will each year have to submit to the Department a statement of transport policies and a costed programme. For 1975/6 see DoE circular 60/74.

[**29**] By s. 6 (5) (*a*) and (*b*) the Secretary of State may treat transport expenditure by London borough councils and district councils as the expenditure of the G.L.C. or county. It was explained that this means that proposed expenditure by borough and district councils will rank for grant in so far as it is approved by G.L.C. or county. There is no obligation on the latter to include any particular expenditure incurred by the former.

[**30**] The new grant will replace certain specific grants (see Sch. I, Part II). The power to make grants for unremunerative railway passenger services is not affected.

[**31**] It is the intention that for a few years this new grant will be fixed close to the average of the present specific grants (about 75 per cent.), and that thereafter the new grant will be reduced, the amount by which it is reduced being shifted into the rate support grant, so that eventually about 50 per cent. of transport grant will be in the transport supplementary grant, the other 50 per cent. being in the rate support grant.

NATIONAL PARKS SUPPLEMENTARY GRANT

[**32**] By s. 7 supplementary grants are payable to county councils for National Parks purposes. The aggregate amount, and the method of apportionment between counties are left to be prescribed by the rate support grant order. The amount payable to each county is determined by the Secretary of State by reference to so much of a county's estimated expenditure on National Parks as he, after consulting the Countryside Commission, thinks appropriate.

[**33**] The amendment moved in Committee sought to ensure that that proportion should be not less than 75 per cent. It was argued that the previous practice of paying a 75 per cent. grant should be made statutory. The Government, while saying that it was intended to pay at least that proportion in future, would not bind itself in the way proposed; the 75 per cent. grant would be of

such expenditure by the local authority as the department thought appropriate.

[**34**] The Minister stated that the money made available for these purposes would cover the full cost of administration including costs attributable to development control, and also management agreements with landowners, not previously covered.

[**35**] The grant is payable to county councils whose areas include the whole or any part of a National Park. An amendment to provide that in the case of the two Parks administered by joint planning boards (Lake and Peak), the grant should be payable directly to them and not via county councils, was not called, but the Minister expressed sympathy for the idea. It was not however possible to amend the Bill to take account of it.

GRANTS FOR RATE REBATE SCHEMES AND STUDENT AWARDS

[**36**] Section 8 curiously sandwiched between sections which deal with the countryside (ss. 7, 9), provides for 90 per cent. grants for statutory rate rebate schemes and local rate rebate schemes, and for mandatory university and teacher training grants. In a brief "clause stand part" debate there was some discussion as to whether these should be 100 per cent. grants. The rebate schemes are discussed in Chapter 2, *post*.

GRANTS AND LOANS BY THE COUNTRYSIDE COMMISSION

[**37**] Section 9 replaces s. 5 of the Countryside Act 1968. Under that section the Countryside Commission could give financial assistance only to persons other than public bodies, and only in respect of projects approved by the Minister. Those limitations are removed, and to that extent greater freedom is given to the Commission. However, assistance given is still, as in the 1968 Act, to be "in accordance with arrangements approved by the Secretary of State and the Treasury," and the Secretary of State retains control through the power to give directions to the Commission.

[**38**] The arrangements or guidelines within which the Commission is to operate are (i) its responsibilities are principally national parks, and other key areas such as areas of outstanding natural beauty, green belts, (ii) the rapid provision of more facilities for informal recreation, particularly on the fringes of big cities, (iii) the encouragement of higher standards of management and design, (iv) the development of the understanding of the countryside and of the needs of townsmen and countrymen.[12]

[**39**] By Part III of Sch. I to the Act grants are no longer payable under the National Parks and Access to the Countryside Act 1949, s. 97 (with exceptions) or 98 of the Local Government Act 1966, s. 8 or 10, of the Countryside Act 1968, s. 33, 34 or 35.

---

[12] H. of C. Official Report, S.C.A., 4th December 1973, col. 232.

CHAPTER TWO

RATING

[**40**] Part II of the Act deals with rating. A new rate rebate scheme is introduced; the law relating to the rating of unoccupied property is amended; a compulsory surcharge on unused commercial property is introduced; the exemption for facilities for disabled persons is extended; the rules for ascertaining the net annual value of certain hereditaments are altered, and the Minister's power in respect of the rating of plant and machinery and of certain public utlities is amended. Finally, it provides that valuation lists are not to be altered on account of central heating installations and minor structural alterations.

[**41**] Expressions used in this part of the Act are, except as otherwise provided, to be given the same meanings as in "the principal Act"—*i.e.*, the General Rate Act 1967.

THE STATUTORY RATE REBATE SCHEME

[**42**] Section 11 provides that the Secretary of State is to make a statutory rate rebate scheme for the grant to residential occupiers of rate rebates. The definition of residential occupier is in s. 13.

[**43**] The scheme is to have effect in respect of rebate periods beginning on or after 1st April 1974. Rebate period is defined in s. 11 (4). In the Bill the phrase "being a part of a year" appeared after the word "period" but it was deleted in Committee. The purpose and effect of the deletion was to make it possible for a period to apply to the second half of one year and the first half of the next.

[**44**] Explaining the need for a new scheme, the Minister referred to the defects of the then current scheme and the way the new scheme would seek to eliminate them. It would be less inflexible, less indiscriminate and would apply to 2 million people, compared with 800,000 under the then scheme. It would also be linked to the rent rebate scheme. The loss of rate income could be, he thought, of the order of £90m (s. 8 (1) (*a*) provides a central grant of 90 per cent.). For the current scheme see S.I. 1974 No. 411.

LOCAL RATE REBATE SCHEMES

[**45**] Section 12 enables a rating authority to make a local rate rebate scheme. It may be distinct from or may merely consist of variations of the statutory scheme. However, it is subject to these constraints. It must be so framed that, in the view of the authority (i) for any rebate period no person will be entitled under the scheme to a rebate less than that to which he would be entitled under the statutory scheme, (ii) the total of the rebates will not in any

year exceed the permitted total for that year. This permitted total is for any area 110 per cent. of the total that would have been allowable under the statutory scheme if it had been in force. The Minister said of this provision "I can conceive of its being something of a charter for those on small fixed incomes in, say, seaside resorts. Let us take a community that has a new and active port—it could be Felixstowe or somewhere like that—with substantial revenues from the industrial installations . . . That local authority may judge that the group of people—for example, seaside landladies—who have been living on relatively small incomes and who have been shocked by the rates over the years ought to be eligible for something better than the statutory scheme. That local authority may feel, in the light of its total revenue situation, that it is able to put in a better scheme. There is nothing to stop it."[1] However, any such generosity over and above the statutory scheme is for the authority itself as the 90 per cent. central grant is of the rebates that would be granted under the statutory scheme (s. 8 (1) (*b*)).

[**46**] When a rating authority passes a resolution making (or varying or revoking) a local scheme, it must send a copy of the resolution to the Secretary of State.

[**47**] It will be noted that a local scheme must be so framed that in the view of the authority it will comply with the two limitations referred to above. The Act does not leave the matter there. The authority must, within the time required by the Act, send to the Secretary of State a certificate specifying the total amount of rebates allowed and the permitted total. Where the former exceeds the latter the authority must convey to the Secretary of State, with the certificate, their proposals for varying or revoking their scheme so as to ensure that in the year following that to which the certificate relates the same thing will not happen again. If they think no change is necessary to ensure that, they must give their reasons for so thinking.

[**48**] If the Secretary of State disagrees, that is, if he thinks the proposals will not have the intended effect, or that some change to the scheme is necessary, he can provide that the scheme (a) shall be subject to such variations as he specifies; or (b) shall be revoked.

[**49**] But what of the first limitation on a local scheme, referred to above (para. [**45**]), namely, that it must be so framed that no one will get less rebate under it than he would under the statutory scheme? If it comes to the knowledge of the Secretary of State that that condition is not fulfilled in respect of *any* person, he may order the variation or revocation of the scheme as in (a) and (b) above.

ELIGIBILITY FOR RATE REBATES

[**50**] Residential occupiers, as defined in s. 13 are entitled to rebates. The present form of sub-s. (1) (*b*) is due to an amendment in Committee. In the original form of the subsection eligibility depended on the hereditament being used mainly for purpose of a private dwelling. Further, one was excluded from rebate if the rateable value of the hereditament *as a whole* was over the "specified limit". The amendment deleted those limitations. The intention was to bring

[1] H. of C. Official Report, S.C.A., 4th December 1973, col. 251.

more small shopkeepers who live over the shop within the rebate scheme than was possible under the previous scheme. Subsection (1) (*c*) enables a tenant or subtenant to have rate rebates.

[**51**] Where a local scheme is in operation, one is not eligible for a rebate under the statutory scheme. However, if one can show that one is entitled to a lesser rebate under the local than under the statutory scheme, one can apply for the statutory rebate. Where any such application is made for any rebate period one then ceases to be eligible to apply under the local scheme for that period.

[**52**] Section 14 (3) deals with the case where an occupier is entitled to a rebate and is also given relief on the grounds of poverty under s. 53 of the General Rate Act.

[**53**] For the "specified limits", see S.I. 1974 No. 412.

RATING OF UNOCCUPIED PROPERTY

[**54**] Under the previous law an authority had discretion by resolution to impose rating of 50 per cent. on empty property. But the system was inflexible in many ways: the resolution could apply only to the whole of the authority's area; it could not apply to classes of hereditaments, only to all; and it had to have effect for seven years. Section 15 removes these limitations. There is power to rate up to 100 per cent.; property can be rated by classes; properties in a part only of an authority's area can be rated; and a resolution can be passed or rescinded at any time.

[**55**] Amendments were moved to make possible penal rating above 100 per cent. The Minister said that while the amendments as they stood were not satisfactory, he was prepared to consider the matter. Accordingly a new clause providing for such rating was moved at the Report stage by the Minister. It is now s. 16, which adds two new sections, 17A and 17B to the General Rate Act 1967. The sections are reasonably self-explanatory. Section 17 (A) (1) imposes on the owner of a commercial building a surcharge additional to any rates (including those imposed under the provision referred to above). It is payable where for a continuous period exceeding six months the building is not used for the purpose for which it was constructed or adapted.

Note: (i) This is not a discretionary scheme, unlike that mentioned in para. [**54**] above.

(ii) Owner is defined in s. 17B (7).

(iii) Commercial building is defined in s. 17B (2). Residential accommodation and industrial premises are excluded. (The Minister justified this on the ground that they did not constitute a comparable mischief, and in any case, compulsory purchase powers were available for residential accommodation left empty.) Warehouses are included.

(iv) To prevent avoidance by short term letting arrangements, s. 17B (4) provides that where the building is used for a period of less than six weeks, that period is ignored in determining the continuous period.

(v) A building is "used" if only four-fifths of it is used for the relevant purposes.

(vi) The sections came into force on 8th February 1974 but do not operate retrospectively.

[56] What is the amount of surcharge? Section 17A (3) states how it is to be calculated where the owner is in rateable occupation; 17A (4) where he is not.

[57] However, no surcharge is payable in either of two circumstances. The first is where the owner has tried his best to let the building. This seems a somewhat colloquial phrase to use in an Act of Parliament, but is it not equivalent to and more agreeable than the more common "uses his best endeavours"? Section 17A (5) specifies certain factors which, amongst others, are to be taken into account in determining whether the owner has tried his best. It is of course for the rating authority in the first place to decide whether the owner has tried his best. If it thinks he has not, but he thinks he has, then it is open to him to appeal or to resist an action as provided by general rating law.

[58] The second case where a surcharge is not payable is to do with the condition of the building (s. 17A (2) (*b*)).

[59] The opposition moved an amendment which would have empowered rating authorities to impose, with the consent of the Secretary of State, even higher but undefined, penalties. The Minister resisted it on the ground *inter alia* that it would be wrong to give local authorities any discretion as this was a matter of national policy. The surcharge accrues to the local authority. This was criticized on the ground that it is not related to the cost of local government services.

INCREASES IN STATUTORY DEDUCTION FROM GROSS VALUE

[60] It appears that an anomaly was created at the last revaluation in the matter of the narrowing of the gap between gross and net rateable values. The purpose of s. 17 was to ensure that if an order were made under s. 19 (2) of the General Rate Act 1967 to eradicate that anomaly, it could be given speedy effect by requiring the valuation officer to direct the rating authority accordingly.

[61] Such an order was made—see S.I. 1973 No. 2139. The main effect was intended to be to reduce by amounts ranging from £1 to £9 the rateable values of about 10 million dwellings from 1st April 1974.

RATING OF PLANT AND MACHINERY

[62] Section 21 (5) of the General Rate Act 1967 empowers the Minister to exclude certain items of plant and machinery from being treated as part of a hereditament for valuation purposes. The power was exercisable where the item satisfied certain conditions. Section 18 amends those conditions. See now S.I. 1974 No. 413.

RATING OF CERTAIN PUBLIC UTILITIES

[63] Section 19 empowers the Secretary of State to make provision by order for determining the rateable value of hereditaments specified in Sch. 3. These include water undertakings, railway or canal premises, Electricity Board,

Coal Board, Post Office and Gas Corporation hereditaments, mines and quarries, dock or harbour undertakings and wire-diffusion hereditaments. Accordingly, such an order may repeal or amend those provisions of earlier statutes which deal with those matters (see s. 19 (4)). The order is subject to the affirmative Parliamentary procedure.

DISABLED PERSONS' FACILITIES

[**64**] Under s. 45 of the General Rate Act 1967 rating relief is granted in respect of various structures supplied for the use of disabled persons, including garages for invalid vehicles. This exemption relates to the structures but not to the sites on which they are built. Until the 1973 revaluation that distinction created no problem as the sites were of such little value that they were of no significance in the valuation. But that might not be the case now—hence the provisions of s. 20 which extends exemption to the land on which the structure is erected (or to the land on which there is no structure but which is used exclusively for keeping a vehicle of the kind in question).

[**65**] Both in Committee and at the Report stage the opposition moved an amendment to extend the exemption. This disclosed some Ministerial confusion as to what s. 45 already permits, but on taking advice, the Minister stated that it provides exemptions "for matters such as provision of lifts, wider corridors, special doors and other facilities which the disabled may require".[2]

MINOR STRUCTURAL ALTERATIONS

[**66**] Section 21 deals in part with what the Minister called "one of the many irritations of the rating system"—the increase in assessment when central heating is put in. It seeks to remove the irritation by saying that the gross value is not to be increased by reason of structural alterations on or after 1st April 1974 in so far as the alterations are for installing "a system for providing heating in two or more rooms". Thus, as from that date the installation of central heating is to be ignored between revaluations.

[**67**] The same is true of a structural alteration which would otherwise result in an increase in the gross value not exceeding such an amount as the Secretary of State may by order specify. This has been specified as £30—see S.I. 1974 No. 629.

[**68**] Subsections (2), (3) and (4) deal with the case where a structural alteration (other than by installation of central heating) is made and either by agreement, on appeal under s. 76, on arbitration under s. 78 or by decision of the Lands Tribunal appeal under s. 77 (all of the General Rate Act 1967), the increase is such that it does not exceed the amount specified by the Secretary of State, as referred to in the previous paragraph.

[**69**] Subsection (5) deals with the case where there is more than one such structural alteration.

---

[2] H. of C. Official Report 1719.

CHAPTER THREE

COMPLAINTS OF MALADMINISTRATION IN LOCAL GOVENRMENT

THE BACKGROUND

[70] A new complaints machinery for local government is provided in Part III of the 1974 Act. Its history may be briefly traced in this way. The Crichel Down affair of 1954, which involved complaints of misbehaviour by civil servants, had led to the appointment of the Committee on Administrative Tribunals and Enquiries, under the chairmanship of Lord Franks. The Committee was limited by its terms of reference to a consideration of those disputes between citizens and central government departments in which some formal machinery for an enquiry or appeal already existed. The Committee's function was to suggest improvements to that machinery. It pointed out in its Report that "over most of the field of public administration no formal procedure is provided for objecting or deciding on objections".[1]

[71] The Committee's Report was followed by the Tribunals and Inquiries Act 1958, but like the report itself, it did not concern itself with the field of administration where there was no formal procedure for objecting. At about the same time interest began to be shown in this country in the institution of the Ombudsman, and in 1960 *Justice*, the British section of the International Commission of Jurists, appointed a Committee under Sir John Whyatt, to undertake an enquiry into the problem. The terms of reference of the Committee were "to enquire into the adequacy of the existing means for investigating complaints against administrative acts or decisions of government departments and other public bodies, where there is no tribunal or other statutory procedure available for dealing with the complaints; and to consider possible improvements to such means, with particular reference to the Scandinavian institution known as the Ombudsman".

[72] It will be noted that the terms of reference of the *Justice* Committee referred to decisions of government departments "and other public bodies". For various reasons however, the Committee excluded from their enquiry complaints against the Police and against nationalised industries. What of local authorities? The Committee's report said:

> "We have considered complaints against local government authorities, but in view of the vast area covered by local government administration,

---

[1] Report of the Committee on Administrative Tribunals and Enquiries, Cmnd. 218, para. 10.

> we have not felt able to carry our enquiry to the stage where we could make specific recommendations."[2]

The material the Committee gathered was, however, published as Appendix A of their report. In that appendix the Committee wrote:

> "the opinion was expressed by several persons of experience in public affairs whose responsibility and judgment in these matters command respect, that there was probably a serious amount of maladministration in local government, and certainly considerably more than in the central government departments. It is impossible to say how far these opinions are justified, but the fact that they are held by responsible people is, in itself, of some significance."

[73] Confining itself then to maladministration by central government departments the *Justice* Committee recommended the establishment of the office of Parliamentary Commissioner to investigate complaints of maladministration against government departments. It is fair to say that the then Conservative government did not favour the idea: there was in their view no need for such an institution. In 1965 the Labour government published a White Paper setting out its proposal for a Parliamentary Commissioner, and these were given effect in the Parliamentary Commissioner Act 1967. The final paragraph of the White Paper said:

> "In due course it may be desirable to consider extending the powers of the Commissioner to deal with complaints of the private citizen against the administrative action of other public authorities."[3]

[74] The Parliamentary Commissioner is authorised to investigate action taken by or on behalf of the government departments and other authorities listed in the Second Schedule to the 1967 Act. Local authorities are not listed there, so he is unable to investigate the acts of a local authority except where in any particular case it acts on behalf of a government department. (Only one such case appears to have been investigated by the Parliamentary Commissioner.)[4]

[75] Pressure built up from many quarters for the application of the Parliamentary Commissioner principle to local government: Private Members Bills were introduced, *Justice* produced in 1969 a further report recommending "an Ombudsman-like institution to carry out in relation to local government functions similar to those carried out in relation to the central government by the Parliamentary Commissioner";[5] in 1969 a Commissioner for Complaints was established for local government in Northern Ireland;[6] many complaints about local government were being made to the Parliamentary Commissioner only of course to be rejected by him.

---

[2] The Citizen and the Administration, para. 12.

[3] Cmnd. 2767.

[4] See H.C. 42, 1973–74, p. 11, Case C.278/T, concerning motor taxation, and Foulkes, "The Parliamentary Commissioner and Local Authorities", *Local Government Chronicle*, 17 August 1973.

[5] "The Citizen and his Council."

[6] Commissioner for Complaints Act (Northern Ireland) 1969.

[76] A parallel development was that following disclosures of the unsatisfactory state of affairs at certain hospitals, opinion built up in favour of a Health Commissioner to deal with complaints about the Health Service.[7]

[77] In the White Paper "Local Government in England"[8] the government undertook to introduce improved arrangements for investigating complaints of maladministration by local authorities. They had come to accept that a citizen who believes himself to be the victim of maladministration by a local authority should enjoy the same right to have his complaint independently scrutinised as he already enjoys through the Parliamentary Commissioner in respect to alleged maladministration by central government. The complaints machinery in local government is therefore an adaptation of the Parliamentary Commissioner system, and to appreciate it fully it is necessary to know something about the Parliamentary Commissioner.[9] All that need be said at this stage is that he can investigate the action of central government departments in any case where a member of the public makes a written complaint to a member of the House of Commons (not necessarily his own, and not to a member of the Lords) of having suffered injustice in consequence of maladministration, and where the member with the consent of the complainant requests the Commissioner to investigate the complaint. The Commissioner reports the results of his investigation to the complainant, to the member who raised it with him, and also makes annual and special reports to Parliament. The latter contain a full account of a selection of cases dealt with by him including all those where he finds maladministration. If he does find it, he can not order a department to act or to refrain from acting in any way. But he is properly concerned to see that the citizen obtains a remedy, for if he finds maladministration, he will expect the department to provide an appropriate remedy. If the department is unwilling or unable to do so, the Parliamentary Commissioner can report the matter to Parliament. His reports are considered by a Select Committee of the House, and their reports are of considerable influence.

[78] The main problem in introducing the Parliamentary Commissioner concept into local government was to devise a scheme which would take account of the different constitutional relationships in local government. For example, unlike M.P.s, councillors as such partake in executive decisions, and, further, might all be of the same political party. Again, the Parliamentary Commissioner reports to Parliament, and his reports are considered by an all-party Select Committee: to whom should a Local Commissioner report? Another problem was the relationship between the Parliamentary and Local Commissioners, for many complaints, as the Parliamentary Commissioner's Reports show, involve both central and local government, as, for example in the field of planning and education. In other respects the powers and procedures of the Local Commissioners follow closely those of the Parliamentary Commissioner; in many cases the same wording is used in both Acts. We may assume that where this is the case the Local Commissioners will give it the meaning given by the Parliamentary Commissioner. This will be referred to at the appropriate places.

---

[7] See National Health Service Reorganisation Act 1973, Part III.
[8] Cmnd. 4584.
[9] See Foulkes, *Introduction to Administrative Law*, 3rd Edn., pp. 253–263.

THE COMMISSIONS FOR LOCAL ADMINISTRATION

[79] The Act provides[10] that there are to be two Commissions for Local Administration, one the Commission for Local Administration in England, the other the Commission for Local Administration in Wales. Each Commission is a body corporate. The membership of each consists of (i) the Parliamentary Commissioner and (ii) such number of other members, known as Local Comissioners, as may be appointed. Appointment of the latter is by the Crown on the recommendation of the Secretary of State after consultation by him with the appropriate "representative body" referred to below. Local Commissioners may be appointed to serve on a full-time or a part-time basis. (The role of the Parliamentary Commissioner is referred to below.) The Secretary of State designates two of the English Commissioners as Chairman and Vice-Chairman of the English Commission. If there is more than one Local Commissioner in Wales (there must be at least one), one is to be designated Chairman.

[80] A person is disqualified for appointment or for being a Local Commissioner if (i) he is disqualified for election to or being a member of any of the authorities subject to investigation under the Act, or (ii) he is a member of, or by co-option of a committee of any of those authorities. Where a Local Commissioner has been a member of any such authority he may be disqualified from conducting a case relating to it.[11]

[81] A Local Commissioner holds office during good behaviour and may be removed from office by Her Majesty on grounds of incapacity or misbehaviour. He may be relieved of office at his own request and in any case vacates office on completing the year of service in which he becomes sixty-five.

[82] A Local Commissioner can not be a member of the House of Commons. A Local Commissioner while so acting and for three years afterwards is disqualified from accepting any paid office by an authority liable to investigation if the area for which he is or was responsible (see next paragraph) falls wholly or partly within the area for which such authority is responsible.

[83] The investigation of complaints is done by a Local Commissioner not by the Commission. The main function of each Commission is to make the necessary administrative arrangements for running the complaints machinery. Each may appoint a secretary and such other staff as it thinks necessary and must provide accommodation for the Local Commissioners and allocate staff to assist them. The English Commission has to divide England into areas and to arrange for one or more Local Commissioners to be responsible for each area. The same may be done in Wales if there is more than one Local Commissioner. A Local Commissioner may be responsible for more than one area, and the Commission must arrange for Local Commissioners to accept cases for which they are not responsible, *i.e.*, for cases arising outside their area or country: the purpose of these rules is to enable the Commissions to spread the work load.

[84] The Commissions must publish information about the procedures for making complaints. They must every year review the operation of the complaints machinery, and may convey to local authorities and government departments any recommendations or conclusions they arrive at in their review.

---

[10] See generally ss. 23 and 24, Sch. 4.
[11] Sch. 4, para. 1 (2).

[85] The functions of a Local Commissioner except that of making a report may be performed by any officer of the Commission authorised for the purpose by the Commissioner. (In accordance with usual practice this would not seem to require express authorisation.)

[86] The expenses incurred by the English Commission are to be met by the English county councils, the Greater London Council and the Council of the Isles of Scilly. Those incurred by the Welsh Commission are to be met by the Welsh county councils. The method of apportionment amongst authorities is set out in the Act. It will be noted that these expenses fall on certain *local* authorities. We shall see later that it is not only local authorities which can be investigated. The Act therefore goes on to provide that the Secretary of State may by order, made by statutory instrument, provide for some specified part of a Commission's expenses to be met by such authorities, other than local authorities, which are liable to investigation, as he specifies in the order. This provision was added at the Third Reading stage in the Commons.

[87] In each financial year each Commission prepares an estimate of the expenses it will incur in the next financial year and submits it to the appropriate, *i.e.*, the English or Welsh representative body. If the representative body wishes to submit any observations on the estimate to the Commission it must do so within one month of receiving it. The Commission must take such observations into account before taking any final decision affecting their expenditure for the following financial year. And it must within fourteen days of taking any final decision as to the estimate, notify the representative body of the decision. Where, after this procedure has been followed, that body thinks the estimate is excessive, it may refer the question to the Secretary of State. If the Secretary of State thinks that, on the basis of the estimate, the Commission's expenditure is likely to be excessive, he may give to the Commission such direction as he thinks necessary to ensure that it is not excessive. The Commission must of course comply with any such direction.

These provisions as they now stand were arrived at as a result of amendments during the Bill's Parliamentary progress. One purpose of the amendments was to increase the powers of the representative bodies in relation to the Commissions' expenditure.

AUTHORITIES SUBJECT TO INVESTIGATION

[88] (1) The following authorites are subject to investigation[12]

(a) any local authority (This is defined as meaning a county council, the Greater London Council, a district council, a London borough council, the Common Council of the City of London, or the Council of the Isles of Scilly. Thus Parish Councils and, in Wales, Community Councils are not liable to investigation under this provision.);

(b) any joint board the constituent authorities of which are all local authorities;

(c) any police authority, other than the Secretary of State;

(d) any water authority within the meaning of the Water Act 1973.

[12] S. 25.

One of the most strongly pressed amendments to the Bill was the proposal to add rent scrutiny boards, rent assessment panels and rent tribunals to the above list. It was resisted by the Government on the ground that they are not part of local government administration. A proposal to add new town development corporations and the Commission for the New Towns was also resisted.

[**89**] (2) Other authorities may be made subject to investigation as the provisions of the Act may be extended by Order in Council to any authority, established by or under statute, which has power to levy a rate, or to issue a precept. This would include parish and community councils. In the original Bill the words "to a rating authority" appeared after "precept", but they were deleted at the Report stage so as to make it possible to extend the Act to those bodies which issue precepts to a county council. Conservancy authorities were mentioned as an example.

[**90**] Where an authority is being investigated the acts of members and officers may of course be investigaged, as may the acts of any person or body acting for the authority under what are popularly called agency arrangements. The acts of certain committees which local authorities may be empowered or required to establish, or to join with other authorities in establishing, are specifically stated to be included within the meaning of "authority" for this purpose. They are: education committees of local education committees, the special education committee of the Greater London Council, police committees, social services committees, and childrens' regional planning committees.

MATTERS SUBJECT TO INVESTIGATION

[**91**] A Local Commissioner may investigate a complaint made (in the way described below) by a person who claims to have sustained injustice in consequence of maladministration in connection with action taken by or on behalf of the authority, being action taken in the exercise of administrative functions of that authority.[13]

[**92**] The meaning of "injustice" and "maladministration" is discussed at paras. [**118**], [**119**], *post*. At this point the following may be noted—

(i) the section follows the wording of s. 5 (1) of the Parliamentary Commissioner Act.

(ii) "Action" is defined in s. 34 (1) as including failure to act.

(iii) A Local Commissioner may investigate action taken by a body acting on behalf of an authority which can be investigated even though that body when acting in its own behalf cannot be investigated.

(iv) What is meant by "administrative functions?" In the working of the Parliamentary Commissioner Act the phrase has been taken to exclude *legislative* functions and thus the procedure leading up to the making of, and the making of statutory instruments. The Parliamentary Comission will nevertheless ask whether, following complaints of a statutory instrument, the Department has taken the proper steps to review its working. By analogy it seems that the steps leading to the making of and the making of Bye-laws by a local authority are excluded from a Local Commissioner's jurisdiction, but that he could concern himself

[13] S. 26.

with the proper review of the by-laws by the authority. Ministerial statutory orders which are not made by way of statutory instruments are not regarded as falling outside the Parliamentary Commissioner's jurisdiction, and it seems clear that a compulsory purchase order, a closing order, a demolition order or any order similar in nature is made in the exercise of a local authority's administrative functions and would not fall outside the Local Commissioner's jurisdiction on this ground.

What of an authority's *judicial* functions? Are they for this purpose to be contrasted with administrative functions and do they therefore fall outside the Local Commissioner's jurisdiction? There are court decisions in which local authorities' functions have been classified as judicial, but it would not necessarily be proper to apply them here because of the very different contexts. In no case has the Parliamentary Commissioner declined jurisdiction on the sole ground that the act in question was judicial.[14]

MATTERS EXCLUDED FROM INVESTIGATION

Excluded by reason of another remedy

[93] The following are excluded from a Local Commissioner's jurisdiction by s. 26 (6), namely any action in respect of which the person aggrieved—

(a) has or had a right of appeal, reference or review to or before a tribunal constituted by or under any enactment;
(b) has or had a right of appeal to a Minister of the Crown;
(c) has or had a remedy by way of proceedings in any court of law.

The function of Local Commissioners as of the Parliamentary Commissioner, is to provide a means of redress for maladministration where no other means is available or suitable—hence these exclusions.

[94] With regard to (a), "tribunal" is not defined in the Act (except to say that a tribunal can consist of one person).[15] "Tribunal", it has been said, "is an unusually fluid expression".[16] For this purpose we may take it to mean a body not being a Minister or a court of law, and whether or not called a tribunal, which has statutory powers to determine an issue presented to it (whether by way of appeal, reference or review) concerning some act or decision of an authority subject to investigation under this Act. A tribunal has to be distinguished from an inquiry which does not determine an issue. Relevant examples of tribunals are the industrial tribunals and the Lands Tribunal. Rent tribunals and rent assessment committees are tribunals but it is not so clear that rent scrutiny boards are.

[95] Examples of (b) abound. Two are the right of appeal from a refusal of planning permission, and the appeal against a notice served under the Advance Payments Code (Highways Act 1959, s. 193 (5)). A point of interest arises under s. 68 of the Education Act 1944 which provides that a person may complain to the Minister of the unreasonable acts of a local education authority, etc.

---

14 [1974] Public Law, p. 1.
15 S. 34 (1).
16 Wraith & Hutchesson, *Adminstrative Tribunals*, p. 15.

The previous Government's view was that this is not an "appeal" under this paragraph, so that the existence of this procedure does not exclude a complaint to a Local Commissioner.[17]

[**96**] Under (c) is excluded a complaint in respect of which there is a remedy by way of common law proceedings, *e.g.*, a complaint of personal injury caused by the negligently maintained school premises. Also excluded is a complaint of a matter in respect of which statute permits an appeal or other reference to a court, *e.g.*, a decision of a local authority altering the name of a street (Public Health Act 1925, s. 18). Where the statute provides that objection to a proposed scheme may be put to a local authority, and that the authority may then refer the matter to a court to have objections adjudicated on,[18] the complaint would not, it seems, be excluded as the proceedings may only be brought by the authority. Contrast a complaint about charges for the collection of trade refuse: application to the court in the matter may be made by either party, so that a complaint to a Local Commissioner would be excluded.[19]

[**97**] However, there is a proviso to s. 26 (6) now being considered. It is that a Local Commissioner may conduct an investigation notwithstanding the existence of a right or remedy referred to in paras. (a) (b) or (c) above, if he is satisfied that in the particular circumstances it is not reasonable to expect the person to resort or have resorted to it.

[**98**] Paras. (a) and (c) above together with the proviso, are in the Parliamentary Commissioner Act. In no case where there was a right of appeal to a tribunal has the Parliamentary Commissioner acted under the proviso. He has done so where proceedings might have been brought before a court, for example where the complainant had not enough money to sustain legal proceedings and could not get legal aid, and where the law on the point was not clear. Presumably the Local Commissioners will act along the same lines. A not uncommon ground for complaint is that the complainant was given incorrect advice by a civil servant. Such complaints have not been excluded by the Parliamentary Commissioner on the ground of the availability of a legal remedy.

Matters excluded by Schedule 5

[**99**] Schedule 5 to the Act lists a number of matters which are not subject to investigation. They are set out in five paragraphs to the Schedule as follows.

[**100**] (i) The commencement or conduct of civil or criminal proceedings in any court of law.

The same wording appears in the Parliamentary Commissioner Act, and under it the Commissioner has declined to investigate a complaint of the refusal of a Department to institute proceedings.

[**101**] (ii) Action taken by any authority in connection with the investigation or prevention of crime.

Thus while a police authority may be investigated, action taken by it in that connection is excluded. The Home Secretary is of course outside a

[17] H. of C. Official Report, S.C.A., 6th December 1973, col. 346.
[18] *E.g.*, Highways Act 1959, s. 178.
[19] Public Health Act 1936, s. 73.

Local Commissioner's jurisdiction but falls under that of the Parliamentary Commissioner. The Parliamentary Commissioner has said however that the Home Secretary as police authority "has no administrative functions which I can investigate in relation to actions taken by the Metropolitan Police for the prevention and investigation of crime."[20] One possible area for complaint to a Local Commissioner (or in the case of the Metropolitan Police to the Parliamentary Commissioner) would be as to the obligation of the police authority to keep themselves informed of the way in which complaints from members of the public are dealt with by the chief officer of police.

[**102**] (iii) Action taken in matters relating to contractual or other commercial transactions.

The same exclusion appears in the Parliamentary Commissioner Act. The justification given there was that the office of Parliamentary Commissioner is to do with relations between government and governed, so that it was proper to exclude him from an area in which the government appears in a different guise—as a trader. The same justification would be made here. A complaint about the opening of tenders would seem to be excluded by this provision.

Some matters are specifically stated to be included in this particular category, and therefore not to be subject to investigation—namely, all transactions relating to (a) the operation of public passenger transport, (b) the carrying on of a dock or harbour undertaking, (c) the provision of entertainment, and (d) the provision of industrial establishments and of markets.

Some matters are specifically stated to be excluded from this category (*i.e.*, are not excluded from investigation as being to do with contractual or other commercial transactions)—viz. (a) transactions for or relating to the organisation or disposal of land, and (b) all transactions (other than those set out at (a) to (d) above) in the discharge of functions exercisable under any public general Act, but excluding those transactions required for the procurement of the goods and services necessary to discharge those functions.

These rules are set out in the Act in a rather convoluted way. As the Minister put it, they are "a series of negatives which require a great deal of threading through to obtain the ultimate sense". It must be remembered that Schedule 5 (being discussed here) itself consists of a list of exceptions. Therefore to find out whether a particular matter can be investigated, one first has to decide whether it falls within the Local Commissioner's jurisdiction as described in paras. [**91**], [**92**], *ante* ("matters subject to investigation"). If it does not, then one need go no further. If it does one has to consider Schedule 5 (amongst other things). The matters excluded or not excluded by the paragraph now being considered, can be set out in this way:

Excluded—Action taken in matters relating to contractual or other commercial transactions, including transactions relating to passenger transport, dock and harbour undertakings, entertainments, industrial establishments and markets. The latter are excluded as being basically of a commercial nature.

---

[20] H.C. 6, 1967–68, para. 25.

Not excluded

(i.e., can be investigated provided they fall under "matters subject to investigation", above)

—Land transactions

—Anything done to discharge any functions under any public general Act except the procurement of goods and services required for the discharge of those functions. The procurement of goods, etc., is excluded because it involves commercial or contractual transactions and thus falls under the main exclusionary principle of this paragraph. It is not clear whether a complaint about the use of a direct labour force is excluded as being to do with the procurement of services.

It might seem unnecessary to exclude from this paragraph anything done under any public general Act, as anything done under such Acts would *prima facie* fall to be investigated. The reason for mentioning it was to make clear that acts done under statutory power are subject to investigation "even if there should be some charging element, such as in the making of charges for accommodation in welfare homes".[21] It was the Government's view therefore that payment for such services does not make them contractual or commercial in nature.

[**103**] (iv) Action taken in respect of appointments or removals, pay, discipline or other personnel matters.

A similar exclusion appears in the Parliamentary Commissioner Act and the Government rejected a suggestion from the Select Committee that it should be removed, arguing that such matters are best dealt with by other and accepted procedures.

[**104**] (v) Any action taken by a local education authority in the exercise of functions under s. 23 of the Education Act 1944.

This says that in general secular instruction is to be under the control of the local education authority. This includes power to determine the times of school sessions, of school holidays, etc.

Also excluded is any action concerning (a) the giving of instruction whether secular or religious or (b) conduct, curriculum, internal management or discipline whether in any school or any college of education or of further education maintained by the authority. In its Consultation Document the Government expressed the view that "the complexities of the distribution of powers and duties between the bodies involved in the education process, and the importance of assuring teachers that their professional activities are not to become subject to inappropriate investigation have led [us] to conclude that it is necessary to limit the Commissioners' jurisdiction over the internal affairs of schools and colleges".

The broad effect of the exclusions is to rule out investigation of complaints about how and what pupils are taught and about the rules and conduct of the

[21] 867 H. of C. Official Report 1762.

institution, including punishment of pupils ("any action concerning . . . conduct . . . or discipline"). Matters which could be investigated include choice of school and selection procedures, the physical condition of a school, school transport, school meals service, students awards. Note also that where the Secretary of State is involved whether on these matters or otherwise a complaint may lie to the Parliamentary Commissioner.

[105] Schedule 5 can be amended by Order in Council so as to *exclude* from it any actions or matters specified in the Order.

Matters excluded by reason of generality of decision

[106] A further exclusionary provision is found in s. 26 (7). This provides that a Local Commissioner is not to conduct an investigation in respect of any action which in his opinion affects all or most of the inhabitants of the area of the authority concerned. This seems to mean that a complaint must be of action taken only in relation to the complainant, and not in relation to persons generally in the area. For example, it would seem to debar a complaint about general arrangements for the collection of household refuse. If however a trader complained of delay in the collection of trade refuse the fact that other traders were also affected would not debar a Local Commissioner as they would not constitute "all or most" of the inhabitants.

There is no parallel provision in the Parliamentary Commissioner Act, but the Commissioner has refused to consider complaints in so far as they allege maladministration affecting persons other than the complainant.

Matters excluded by time

[107] A complaint cannot be accepted in so far as it is in respect of anything done before 1st April 1974, or in respect of any default or alleged default first arising before that date. (For another time-limit, see para. [**116**], *post.*)

WHO CAN COMPLAIN?

[108] By s. 27 of the Act a complaint may be made by any individual or by any body of persons whether incorporated or not. But the following may not complain:

(a) a local authority or other authority or body constituted for purposes of the public service or of local government, or for the purposes of carrying on under national ownership any industry or undertaking or part of an industry or undertaking;
(b) any other authority or body whose members are appointed by Her Majesty or any Minister of the Crown or government department, or whose revenues consist wholly or mainly of money provided by parliament.

The same wording appears in the Parliamentary Commissioner Act, s. 6, and the Parliamentary Commissioner has ruled that a Water Board is a "body constituted for purposes of the public service". A parish council and community council, while not "a local authority" is "a body constituted for purposes of local government". The phrase referring to bodies under national ownership includes what are commonly known as the nationalised industries—the corporations running the gas, electricity, coal transport and other industries.

[**109**] *A complaint has to be made by "the person aggrieved"*. The aggrieved person is defined in s. 34 (1) as "the person who claims or is alleged to have sustained" injustice. The same wording appears in the Parliamentary Commissioner Act 1967. It means that if *you* suffer an injustice but choose to do nothing about it, *I* cannot complain to a Local Commissioner of it, you must do so yourself. A complaint may of course be submitted on one's behalf by an adviser, *e.g.*, solicitor, accountant, or trade union branch secretary. And the Parliamentary Commissioner will investigate complaints by representative bodies such as a civic society, residents' association, hospital action committee, or even a local ward political party, presumably on the ground that the body is conveying a complaint of the injustice suffered by the individual members severally. Unless of course, which does not always appear to be the case, he considers that the body itself suffered an injustice.

[**110**] The section also provides that where the person by whom a complaint might have been made has died or is for any reason unable to act for himself, the complaint may be made by his personal representative or by a member of his family or by some body or individual suitable to represent him.

[**111**] It will be noted that a complainant does not have to reside in the area of the authority of whose action he is complaining. A foreigner or a prisoner may complain.

HOW IS A COMPLAINT TO BE MADE?

[**112**] For a complaint to be considered it must have been made in writing to a member of the authority, or of any other authority concerned.

A member of a local authority can, of course, complain in his capacity as a member of the public even against his own authority, but he cannot do so direct to a Local Commissioner, only through a member of the authority.

[**113**] The complaint to the member must specify the action alleged to constitute maladministration. This latter requirement was not in the original Bill which was amended in committee. The purpose of the amendment, pressed on behalf of local authority associations, was to meet their fears of a flood of frivolous complaints. The requirement introduced by this amendment is not to be found in the Parliamentary Commissioner Act. There is no need for it, and it may be unfortunate. There is no need for it because it is always open to a Local Commissioner to refuse to investigate a complaint on the ground that in his view it is vexatious or frivolous. It may be unfortunate in that it might have the effect of ruling out a complainant who could not spell out in sufficient detail the maladministration causing the injustice he claims to have suffered. The Parliamentary Commissioner has in fact commented "A complainant is usually specific about the injustice he has sustained but less so about the maladministration which caused injustice . . . the complaint says little about the maladministration."[22]

---

[22] Vol. x, J.S.P.T.L., 101 at 104.

[114] The complaint must be referred to the Local Commissioner, with the consent of the person aggrieved (or the person acting on his behalf), by the member to whom it was made (or by any other person who is a member of any authority concerned) with a request to investigate the complaint. The reason for requiring a complaint to be channeled through a member, just as those to the Parliamentary Commissioner are channeled through Members of Parliament, is to support and emphasise the role of the elected representative in redressing grievances. However, because members are themselves involved in decisions and because they may close ranks in the face of a complaint, the Act goes on to provide in s. 26 (3) that where a member of the authority has been asked to refer the complaint to the Commissioner and has not done so, he can receive the complaint direct from the person aggrieved.

[115] The reference in paras. [**112**] and [**114**] above to "any other authority concerned" seems to be intended to cover the situation where one authority is acting as the agent of another. In that case the complaint could be made to either the principal or the agent.

[116] The complaint must be made to the member within twelve months from the day on which the person aggrieved first had notice of the matters alleged in the complaint, but the Local Commissioner may waive this requirement. Compare s. 6 (3) of the Parliamentary Commissioner Act which imposes a similar time bar and discretion. The Parliamentary Commissioner has said, "My discretion is only to be exercised where an exceptional case has been clearly made out: it is not to be used as a general dispensation. In considering whether a case is exceptional I take account of special circumstances where the rigid application of a twelve months limit might bear harshly on a person who, for example, had been prevented by illness from presenting his complaint or had pursued an alternative course of action in the reasonable expectation of finding a remedy . . . I have not attempted to give a comprehensive definition of "special circumstances". This would be impossible, given the wide variety of complaints that have come to me."[23]

[117] Note that no fees of any kind are payable.

THE SUBSTANCE OF THE COMPLAINT

[118] A person aggrieved is one who claims to have "sustained injustice in consequence of maladministration". The same phrase is used in the Parliamentary Commissioner Act. Neither there nor in this Act are "injustice" or "maladministration" defined. This was a deliberate omission. It was thought better to allow the meaning of the words to be filled out by the processes of case work. The meaning given to them by the Parliamentary Commissioner will undoubtedly be applied by the Local Commissioners. Thus "injustice" includes financial loss caused by a refusal to make a financial grant or an *ex gratia* payment or delay in making a payment, or in granting a licence, in improperly refusing to classify a child as "handicapped" and injury to livestock. It also includes being deprived of an amenity by the partial or total withdrawal of a facility previously available, by the destruction of an attractive view, by a

[23] H.C. 134, 1967–68, paras. 26, 30.

supermarket being allowed to be built well in front of a long standing improvement line, and by the loss of one's land for road-widening. It further includes being unnecessarily inconvienced in the use of one's premises by disturbance caused by public works, being caused unnecesary concern or uncertainty, being deprived of the opportunity to object to or appeal against a decision, and failure to consult. Clearly no actual financial loss has to be shown.

[**119**] The following are shown by the Parliamentary Commissioner's reports to amount to maladministration—delay, failure to take all the relevant facts into account before arriving at a decision or to take irrelevant facts into account, perfunctory consideration of a citizen's case, failure to give advice where this is reasonably required, failure to give the citizen a full explanation of the matter affecting him, giving incorrect advice, disparity of treatment between citizens similarly circumstanced, breach of confidentiality, improper conduct of an authority's official at a public local inquiry, and, where an agency agreement is in force, failure by the principal to ensure that the agent authority carries out the delegated functions properly and in accordance with the agreement.

[**120**] The significance of s. 34 (3) must now be considered. It reads—

> "It is hereby declared that nothing in this Part of this Act authorises or requires a Local Commissioner to question the merits of a decision taken without maladministration by an authority in the exercise of a discretion vested in that authority."

The same wording is to be found in the Parliamentary Commissioner Act, s. 12 (3), and in the National Health Service Reorganisation Act, s. 39 (2).

[**121**] The Parliamentary Commissioner took the view that this meant that he could investigate the administrative processes *leading to* a discretionary decision. He was, he said, in no way concerned with the merits of administrative action, but with the way the department reached its decision. If there was no defect in the processes leading to the decision he was not, he said, competent to question the quality of the decision even if it resulted in manifest hardship. However he was encouraged to go further by the Select Committee on the Parliamentary Commissioner. The Committee said that if he found a decision which judged by its effect appeared to him to be thoroughly bad in quality, he might infer from the quality of the decision that there had been maladministration from the substance of the decision, not only from the procedure.

[**122**] What if he did find a defect in the procedure, what could he do? What indeed can he do if he infers maladministration from the quality of the act? It appears that he can question its merits. What does that mean? It is of the essence of the function of the Parliamentary Commissioner, as it is of the Local Commissioners and of the Health Service Commissioners, that he cannot overrule, reverse or annul any decision. He may ask the authority to look at it again, and may report adversely on them but he has no executive power. What s. 34 (3) says is that if he does not find maladministration, he cannot concern himself with the merits. It is implicit in the Act that if he finds maladministration he can concern himself with the merits to the extent just indicated. But it is not yet clear how far the Commissioner is prepared to find maladministration from the quality of, rather than from the procedures attending, a decision. Complainants should not of course be dissuaded by considera-

tions such as these. The kind of situation in which they might arise would be on a complaint of a refusal to allocate a council house.

PRELIMINARY STEPS BEFORE AN INVESTIGATION IS MADE

[123] Before investigating a complaint a Local Commissioner must, by s. 26 (5), satisfy himself that the complaint has been brought to the notice of the authority by or on behalf of the person aggrieved, and that that authority has been given a reasonable opportunity to investigate and reply to the complaint. To bring a complaint to the notice of a member of the authority is not the same thing as bringing it to the notice of the authority itself. It could however be brought to the notice of the authority by the member acting expressly or presumably impliedly on behalf of the complainant.

[124] Where a Local Commissioner proposes to conduct an investigation, he must, by s. 28, give to the authority concerned and to any person alleged to have taken or authorised the action complained of, an opportunity to comment on any allegations contained in the complaint. It will be noted that we have not yet reached the stage of the investigation proper: as a result of the comments received he may decide not to make an investigation.

[125] If the Commissioner is satisfied that he has jurisdiction and that all the necessary procedural steps have been taken he may then carry out an investgation. He is not bound to do so. The Act says he "may investigate".[24] It further says, in s. 26 (10), that in determining whether to initiate, continue or discountinue an investigation, a Commissioner shall "act at discretion", and that it is for him to say whether a complaint has been "duly made", that is, whether the necessary procedural requirements have been fulfilled. This wording is not quite the same as in the Parliamentary Commissioner Act: the alteration may have been made in an attempt to put it beyond doubt that a Local Commissioner's decision in those particular matters is not reviewable in the courts.

THE CONDUCT OF AN INVESTIGATION

[126] *General rule.* An investigation must be in private. Apart from that "the procedure for conducting an investigation shall be such as the Local Commissioner considers appropriate in the circumstances of the case" (s. 28 (2)).

[127] *Obtaining information.* The Commissioner may obtain information from such persons and in such manner and make such inquiries as he thinks fit. He decides whether any person may be represented by a lawyer or otherwise in the investigation. A trade union, NALGO, suggested that there should be an absolute right of representation, but it was not pressed. It was pointed out that the same provisions appear in the Parliamentary Commissioner Act. The Commissioner seems to take the view that representation would be proper if an investigation got to the stage where it appeared that reputations were at stake.

[128] The Parliamentary Commissioner allows a complainant who is being interviewed by a member of his staff to be accompanied by a friend or adviser if he so wishes: the Member of Parliament concerned can attend in that

[24] See *re Fletcher's Application*, [1970] 2 All E.R. 527 (re Parliamentary Commissioner).

capacity. The Parliamentary Commissioner will not however allow a Member to comment on information given to him, the Commissioner, by the department during his investigation.[25] The same procedure will presumably apply here.

[**129**] The Commissioner has commented that his function is not to operate like a judge, arriving at a finding on the evidence put before him, but to ascertain by active inquiry what the facts were which gave rise to the complaint. The Commissioner's staff have interviewed hundreds of complainants, sometimes in their own homes, but he does not allow them to cross-examine those they have complained of. The Local Commissioners will presumably take the same view of their role.

[**130**] A Local Commissioner may, by s. 29, require any person (whether or not a member or officer of the authority concerned) to furnish information and produce documents. He has the same powers as the High Court in respect of the examination of witnesses and of the production of documents, so that no one can be compelled to give evidence or produce documents which he could not be compelled to give or produce in civil proceedings in the High Court.

[**131**] No exception is made in respect of information concerning communications between the authority and a Government department, and no obligation to maintain secrecy or other restriction on the disclosure of information obtained by or furnished to persons in Crown service, whether imposed by any enactment or by any rule of law, applies to the disclosure of information to a Local Commissioner. The Official Secrets Act 1911 is such an enactment and the obligation of confidentiality imposed on an employee is such a rule of law. As to the so-called "Crown privilege"[26] in respect of the production of documents, etc., this is stated not to apply here. Thus the rule mentioned above that one cannot be compelled to give evidence one could not be compelled to give in the High Court does not apply in these circumstances. In sum, no official information is to be hidden from a Local Commissioner.

[**132**] What sanction is available to a Local Commissioner to ensure compliance? The Act provides, by s. 29 (8), that if any person without lawful excuse obstructs a Local Commissioner or any officer of the Commission, or if he is guilty of any act or omission in relation to an investigation which if that investigation were a proceeding in the High Court, would constitute contempt of court, the Commissioner may certify the offence to the High Court. The High Court may after inquiry, deal with the person charged as if he had committed a contempt of the High Court.

[**133**] A Local Commissioner may obtain advice from any person to assist him in his investigation.

[**134**] *Payment of expenses.* The Local Commissioner may pay to the complainant, to any person who attends or gives information, and to any person whose advice he seeks, expenses and compensation for loss of time, within scales laid down.

[**135**] *The effect of the investigation on the authority.* The Act specifically states in s. 28 (4) that the conduct of an investigation "shall not affect any

---

[25] H.C. 138, Session 1969–70, para. 17.

[26] "So-called", as it is now more correct to refer to privilege from disclosure on the ground of public interest. See *Alfred Crompton Amusement Machines, Ltd.* v. *Commissioners of Customs and Excise*, [1973] 2 All E.R. 1169.

action taken by the authority concerned, or any power or duty of that authority to take further action with respect to any matters subject to the investigation". Thus the fact that an investigation is taking place into a matter does not require the authority to refrain from further considering the matter, to refrain from or to delay implementing any decision already taken, or to reverse any decision. No such action or inaction can lead to proceedings as for contempt of court, referred to at para. [**132**]. The same provision is to be found in the Parliamentary Commissioner Act.

[**136**] As we have seen the Commissioner is properly concerned with unremedied injustice. It could happen that a department takes action during an investigation which might have the effect of making it impossible to provide a remedy should the Commissioner find injustice. He therefore gives departments the opportunity of asking him to expedite his inquiries in cases where the prospect of an early finding by him would help the department to decide whether some postponement of irreversible action is compatible with public policy. But such decision is for the department. "A complainant", the Parliamentary Commissioner has said, "must not expect that he can invoke my investigation as a form of injunction against departmental action which he desires to delay".[27] The same warning must apply to the local government complaints machinery.

REPORTS AND OTHER ACTION ON INVESTIGATIONS

Publication by Commissioner

[**137**] A Local Commissioner must send a report of his investigation to (a) the complainant, (b) the person, if any, who referred the complaint to him, and (c) the authority concerned and any other authority or person alleged to have taken or authorised the action complained of (s. 30).

Where the complaint was referred by a person who was, but has since ceased to be a member, the report is to be sent to the chairman or mayor, as the case may be, of the authority.

If the Local Commissioner decides not to conduct an investigation he is to send a statement of his reasons for not doing so to the above persons.

Content

[**138**] In its original form the Bill provided that a Commissioner might, if he thought fit, prepare a special version of his report which omitted the names of persons mentioned in his complete report. The Act alters the emphasis. It says that apart from identifying the authorities concerned the report shall not mention the name of any person or contain any particulars which are likely to identify any person and can be omitted without impairing the effectiveness of the report. However, the Commissioner can mention such name and particulars if he considers it necessary to do so, after taking into account the interest of the public as well as that of the complainant and others. There is nothing in the Parliamentary Commissioner Act on this matter, but it is the Commissioner's practice to "anonymise" his ordinary reports.

---

[27] H.C. 129, 1968–69, para. 25.

Publicity by the authority

[**139**] The authority is required to make copies of the report available for inspection by the public for a period of three weeks. The report is to be available for inspection without charge at all reasonable hours at one or more of their offices. Any person is entitled to take copies of or extracts from the report when it is so available (s. 30).

Public notice must of course be given of the availability of the report for inspection and copying. On receiving the report from the Commissioner therefore the authority's "proper officer"[28] must give such notice as the Act prescribes. The notice must specify the future date from which the three weeks will run. It is an offence to obstruct a person seeking to inspect, etc., the report.

The Local Commissioner can however, direct that a particular report shall not be subject to the above requirements as to publicity by the authority. Nothing in the Act deals with the publication of the report by the complainant or by the person who referred the complaint to him. There is no reason why such persons should not give publicity to the report.

Additional action on a finding of maladministration

[**140**] If in his report a Local Commissioner states that injustice was caused to the person aggrieved in consequence of maladministration, further steps have to be taken (s. 31). The report must be laid before[29] the authority, and it is then it's duty to consider it and to notify the Commissioner of the action they have taken or propose to take.

A number of possibilities then arise—

(a) The Commissioner is notified of the action taken, and is satisfied with it.
(b) He is notified of the proposed action which appears to him to be satisfactory, and later, that that action has been taken.
(c) He does not within a reasonable time receive from the authority notification of action taken or proposed.
(d) Having been notified of the action taken, the Commissioner is not satisfied with it.
(e) Having been notified of proposed action he does not within a reasonable time receive confirmation from the authority that they have taken that proposed action to his satisfaction.

In cases (a) and (b) no further action is called for.

In (c), (d) and (e) the Commissioner is to make a "further report". The provisions above referred to relating to publication of the report, its contents and its availability for inspection then apply.

It is implicit in the above that if the Commissioner receives notification of proposed action but is not satisfied that it will meet the case, he may indicate his dissatisfaction at that stage.

[**141**] To report is the extent of the Commissioner's power on an adverse finding. He cannot order an authority to act or to refrain from acting, to speed up or delay action, to make any payment, to grant a licence. The same is true

[28] *I.e.*, the officer appointed for this purpose. See Local Government Act 1972, s. 270 (3).
[29] Not defined. Does it mean formally presented at a council meeting, with a copy available for every member?

of the Parliamentary Commissioner. Both Parliamentary and Local Commissioners are properly concerned with the remedying of injustice. If the Parliamentary Commissioner finds maladministration causing injustice he will ask the department what remedy they propose. If he does not think it would be adequate he will say so, and expect to receive further proposals. The Local Commissioners will doubtless act in the same way. The granting of a remedy is sought to be ensured through the influence of their respective offices.

Annual Report

[**142**] In addition to the report to be made by a Local Commissioner on each investigation undertaken, each Local Commissioner is also to prepare for every year ending 31st March a general report on the exercise of his functions and to submit it to his Commission (or where he has acted for another Commission to that Commission). The report is to be submitted by 31st May in each year.

Disclosure of information by Commissioners

[**143**] (a) *General prohibition on disclosure.* Information obtained by a Local Commissioner (or an officer of a Commission) in or for an investigation is not to be disclosed. The exceptions are: (i) disclosure for the purposes of an investigation and of any report or further report; (ii) disclosure for the purposes of proceedings for an offence under the Official Secrets Act committed in respect of information obtained by a Commissioner or an officer of a Commission, for an offence of perjury committed in the course of an investigation; (iii) disclosure for the purposes of contempt proceedings in the High Court (s. 32).

[**144**] (b) *Evidence in proceedings.* A Local Commissioner and officers of a Commission are not to be called upon to give evidence in any proceedings of matters coming to his or their knowledge in the course of an investigation. Proceedings under (ii) and (iii) in the above paragraph are excluded from this.

[**145**] (c) *Restriction on disclosure imposed by authorities.* We have seen that a Local Commissioner cannot be denied access to any documents or information (paras. [**130**], [**131**], *ante*). He may however, be prevented from disclosing it in his report or otherwise. By s. 32 (3) any of the authorities liable to investigation under this Act, and a Minister of the Crown (which includes for this purpose the Commissioner of Customs and Excise and Commissioners of Inland Revenue) may give written notice to a Local Commissioner that the disclosure of a particular document or piece of information or of a class of documents or information would be contrary to the public interest. Where such a notice is given such document or information is not to be communicated by anyone for the purposes of an investigation under the Act. However, any notice given by any of the authorities referred to above may be discharged by the Secretary of State. This is presumably in case of over-eager use of the power to prevent disclosure. Further, the notice does not affect the obligation imposed by the Act to give a Local Commissioner information concerning communications between an authority and any Government department. But where information is obtained from such a communication which has not up to that point been made public, certain restrictions on the disclosure of that information are

imposed on the Local Commissioner. (Compare Parliamentary Commissioner Act, s. 11.)

[**146**] The rules in the Parliamentary Commissioner Act, the National Health Service Reorganisation Act and this Act relating to the restriction on disclosure by the respective Commissioners do not apply when those Commissioners are consulting one another under the provisions of this Act mentioned below.

Defamation in relation to investigations under this Act

[**147**] Section 32 provides that the publication of certain matter is absolutely privileged, namely the publication of any matter—

(i) in communications between a *member* of an authority and a Local Commissioner or any officer of either Commission;

(ii) by a Local Commissioner (or any such officer) in communicating with a *complainant*;

(iii) in preparing, making and sending a *report* (or a "further report") *of an investigation* (or a statement of reasons for not investigating), or in making a report available to the public except, in that case, where a Local Commissioner has directed that a report is not to be available for public inspection; and

(iv) contained in a *report* by a Local Commissioner which is made available to the public by being included in a report made by a *representative body*.

It will be noted that communications between a complainant and member, from complainant to Local Commissioner, and publication of a report by member or complainant are not within the above, and do not therefore have the protection of absolute privilege. Other defences might of course be available.

THE REPRESENTATIVE BODIES

Constitution

[**148**] One of the trickiest questions in connection with the establishing of the complaints machinery in local government was this. The Parliamentary Commissioner makes annual (and other) Reports to Parliament on the working of his office: to whom should the Commissioners for England and Wales report? As this is an aspect of local government administration reports to Parliament would be inappropriate.

The Act seeks to meet the difficulties by providing for two representative bodies, one for England, one for Wales, which are intended to represent in their respective countries the authorities to which the Act applies. They are to be designated by order (made by statutory instrument) made by the Secretary of State.[30]

At the Committee stage an amendment was moved which was intended to enable local authority associations designated by the Secretary of State to appoint one (not two) representative body themselves, but it was withdrawn.

Functions

[**149**] For each year ending 31st March each Commission is to prepare a

[30] See S.I. 1974 Nos. 683 and 707 for English and Welsh representative bodies respectively.

general report on the discharge of its functions and to submit it to the English or Welsh Representative Body, as the case may be. The reports are to be submitted "as soon as may be" (which seems to mean as soon as reasonably possible) after the Commissions have received from Local Commissioners the general report they are, as noted above, to submit to the Commissions, and the Commissions must send copies of the Local Commissioners' reports to the representative body, along with their own. The representative body must then publish the reports submitted to them.

As we have seen, the Commissioners may convey to local authorities, through the appropriate representative body, any recommendations or conclusions they may reach in the course of their annual review of the working of the complaint machinery. In transmitting these recommendations or conclusions to local authorities, the representative bodies may make such comments on them as they think fit. Further, when publishing a report submitted to it, a representative body may comment on it and publish their comments in an annex to the report.

To understand how complaints are being handled it will be necessary to have access to the reports made by Local Commissioners to authorities on their investigations. Such reports can be seen at the offices of the authority in question, but this will not be enough. It is important therefore that the general reports submitted to the Commission by the Local Commissioner contain details of specific cases, as do those of the Parliamentary Commissioner to Parliament, so that when published by the representative body they will be generally available, not merely in the area of the particular authorities.

RELATIONSHIP WITH THE PARLIAMENTARY COMMISSIONER

[**150**] It was recognised at an early stage in discussions that arrangements would have to be made to deal with the not infrequent situation where both local and central government, *i.e.*, Local and Parliamentary Commissioners are involved. Since then the office of Health Service Commissioner has been created.

[**151**] What does the Act provide? First, as we have seen, the Parliamentary Commissioner is a member of the English and Welsh Commissions for Local Administration. He does not undertake investigations into complaints under this Act, but rather acts as an adviser to the Local Commissioners. This should help to ensure consistency of judgment. Second, it provides in s. 33 that if at any stage in the course of conducting an investigation a Local Commissioner forms the opinion that the complaint relates partly to a matter which could be the subject of an investigation by the Parliamentary Commissioner or by a Health Service Commissioner he must consult with that Commissioner about the complaint. Such consultation may be about any matter relating to the complaint including the conduct of the investigation and the form, content and publication of any report of the results of the investigation.

[**152**] The Parliamentary Commissioner and a Health Service Commissioner is under a like obligation to consult with the appropriate Local Commissioner where he finds that the complaint he is investigating relates partly to a matter which could be investigated under the 1974 Act.

[**153**] Note what the Act does not provide: it does not provide that where a complaint involves both local and central government both aspects may be investigated by either a Local or the Parliamentary Commissioner. The Parliamentary Commissioner had hoped that this might have been possible, but it has proved otherwise.

[**154**] Thus if say a Local Commissioner is investigating a complaint and thinks it should also be investigated by the Parliamentary or a Health Service Commissioner it will be necessary for the complainant to set in motion the machinery for investigation by the appropriate Commissioner. How is the complainant to know about this? The Local Commissioner has to tell him. A like obligation is put on the Parliamentary Commissioner and a Health Service Commissioner when investigating complaints under their respective Acts. This seems a very awkward arrangement but probably follows inevitably from the principle that this complaints machinery must be geared into local government administration and be seen to be a thing apart from the Parliamentary Commissioner system. Perhaps after some years' experience of the working of these three methods of investigating complaints it will be found possible to amalgamate them.

CHAPTER FOUR

MISCELLANEOUS

RELAXATION OF MINOR CONTROLS

[155] Section 35 removes a number of controls over local authorities found in twenty-six Acts. The details are in Schedule 6. Some of them deal with certain fees payable on the grant of licences: in respect of those, authorities will be able in future to charge such fees as they think appropriate, rather than those fixed by statute; or maxima are abolished. In other cases the form of certain records will not be subject to ministerial direction, and certain acts will not be subject to ministerial consent or direction, for example in planning and road traffic regulation matters.

Highway authorities can now temporarily restrict the use of a road for three months, not six weeks as before. The Opposition doubted the wisdom of the abandonment of certain controls relating to National Parks, etc. (para. 6 (2) and (4) of the Schedule).

Two points may be noted, first, the wider definition in s. 35 (6) of local authority; second, that the Secretary of State may by order remove *any* ministerial control over any local authority function.

ESTABLISHMENT CHARGES

[156] Section 36 was added to the Bill by the Government at the Report stage. Under certain statutes local authorities may recover from a defaulter the cost of doing certain works, and in addition a further five per cent. as establishment charges. This section authorises them to recover, instead of the fixed five per cent. "such sum as appears to them to be reasonable". To the objection that this would introduce uncertainty the Minister said, "I understand that the term 'establishment charges' or 'overheads' is well understood in the building and construction industry, and we would expect local authorities to follow professional practice in these matters."[1] The reasonableness of a local authority's action in this as in other matters is in any event reviewable by the courts.

Note that "local authority" has the same wider meaning as in s. 35.

POWER TO MAKE ADVANCES

[157] Section 37 was also added at the Report stage; the credit is entirely due to an opposition member. It operates by amending s. 43 of the Housing (Financial Provisions) Act 1958. Accordingly it is now possible for an authority to lend money to a mortgagor to enable him to pay off his mortgage, and then

[1] 867 H. of C. Official Report 1537.

to remortgage the property at more acceptable rates of interest. It can do this where satisfied that the primary effect of the advance will be to meet the housing needs of the applicant by enabling him either to retain an interest in the house or to carry out conversion, repairs, etc. This power could also be used to lend money to a wife who, on separation or divorce, gets possession of the house but finds it necessary to buy out the husband's interest. The amendment also makes clear what was previously doubtful, that an authority can grant low-start mortgages. Another example mentioned[2] was a widow whose interest on her mortgage is paid by the Department of Health and Social Security: the property has fallen into some disrepair but does not qualify for an improvement grant. Here again an advance could be made for the repairs to be carried out. Subsection (5) means that an advance can be made in respect of a house over a shop.

WATER CHARGES: RECOVERY BY LOCAL AUTHORITIES

[158] Section 38 was yet another section added to this Bill whilst on its progress through the Commons, in this case in Committee.

It inserts a new section, 32A, in the Water Act 1973. It empowers a local authority and a water authority to enter into an agreement whereby the former may not only collect but also recover on behalf of the latter, charges due to the latter. Rate demand notes will be amended accordingly. (See also Sch. 7, para. 14.)

COMPENSATION FOR LOSS OF OFFICE

[159] Section 39 substitutes a new subsection for s. 259 (3) of the Local Government Act 1972, extending the cases for which regulations for compensation for loss of office may provide.

CLASSIFICATION OF HIGHWAYS

[160] Section 40 provides for the effect on the classification of highways of the discontinuance from 1st April 1975 of grant under the Highways Act 1959 towards the cost of building or improving principal roads. (See paras. [**26**], [**30**], *ante*; see also Sch. 1, para. 6 (*a*), Sch. 7, para. 2.)

MINOR AND CONSEQUENTIAL AMENDMENTS

[161-200] These are listed in Sch. 7. Some have already been referred to. Para. 11 is intended to remove any doubts there may have been as to whether employees of the London Transport Executive are disqualified for election to the G.L.C. They are not.

For a ministerial explanation of para. 12, see H. of C. Official Report, S.C.A., 6th December 1973, col. 379.

Note that by para. 7, the 2½ per cent. limit on the discount allowable for prompt payment of rates is abolished.

---

[2] 867 H. of C. Official Report 1541.

THE LOCAL GOVERNMENT ACT 1974

(1974 c. 7)

ARRANGEMENT OF SECTIONS

PART I

GRANTS

Rate support grants

PART IV

MISCELLANEOUS AND GENERAL

An Act to make further provision, in relation to England and Wales, with respect to the payment of grants to local authorities, rating and valuation, borrowing and lending by local authorities and the classification of highways; to extend the powers of the Countryside Commission to give financial assistance; to provide for the establishment of Commissions for the investigation of administrative action taken by or on behalf of local and other authorities; to restrict certain grants under the Transport Act 1968*; to provide for the removal or relaxation of certain statutory controls affecting local government activities; to make provision in relation to the collection of sums by local authorities on behalf of water authorities; to amend section* 259 (3) *of the Local Government Act* 1972 *and to make certain minor amendments of or consequential on that Act; and for connected purposes* [8th February 1974]

PART I

GRANTS

Rate support grants

1. Rate support grants

(1) Subject to the provisions of this Part of this Act, the Secretary of State shall, for the year 1974–75 and each subsequent year, make grants to local authorities in England and Wales in accordance with this section; and any grants made in pursuance of this subsection shall be known as "rate support grants".

(2) For the purpose of fixing the estimated aggregate amount of the rate support grants for any year, the Secretary of State shall determine the aggregate amount (in this Part of this Act referred to as "the amount available for grants") which he estimates is to be available for the payment out of money provided by Parliament of grants, other than housing subsidies and grants under section 8 below, to local authorities in respect of their relevant expenditure for that year, and shall deduct therefrom—

(*a*) the portion of the amount available for grants which he estimates will be allocated to grants in respect of specific services, other than grants under section 8 below; and

(*b*) the portion of that amount which is prescribed as the aggregate amount of supplementary grants for transport purposes, within the meaning of section 6 below; and

(*c*) the portion of that amount which is prescribed as the aggregate amount of supplementary grants under section 7 below;

and so much of the amount available for grants as remains after making those deductions shall be the estimated aggregate amount of the rate support grants for that year.

(3) Before determining the amount available for grants and the portions of that amount mentioned in paragraphs (*a*) to (*c*) of subsection (2) above, the Secretary of State shall consult with such associations of local authorities as appear to him to be concerned and with any local authority with whom consultation appears to him to be desirable, and shall take into account—

(*a*) the latest information available to him as to the rate of relevant expenditure;

(*b*) any probable fluctuation in the demand for services giving rise to relevant expenditure, so far as the fluctuation is attributable to circumstances prevailing in England and Wales as a whole which are not under the control of local authorities;

(*c*) the need for developing those services and the extent to which, having regard to general economic conditions, it is reasonable to develop those services; and

(*d*) the current level of prices, costs and remuneration and any future variation in that level which in the opinion of the Secretary of State will result from decisions which appear to him to be final and which will have the effect of increasing or decreasing any particular prices, costs or remuneration.

(4) Subject to subsection (6) below, in this section "relevant expenditure", in relation to any year, means the expenditure for that year falling to be defrayed out of the rate fund of a local authority—

(*a*) reduced by the amount of any payments of such descriptions as the Secretary of State may determine which fall to be made for that year into the rate fund; and

(*b*) exclusive of the items of expenditure specified in subsection (5) below.

(5) The items of expenditure referred to in subsection (4) (*b*) above are—

(*a*) sums falling to be paid to another local authority by virtue of a precept or other instrument;

(*b*) expenditure under section 1 (1) (awards for university and comparable courses) or section 2 (3) (grants to persons undergoing training as teachers) of the Education Act 1962; and (*c*) so much of the allowances granted in the year in question under a local authority's allowance scheme, within the meaning of Part II of the Housing Finance Act 1972, as does not exceed the authority's standard amount of rent allowances, within the meaning of that Act, for that year.

(6) The following grants for specific services, namely grants—

(*a*) to the Receiver for the Metropolitan Police District under section 77 of the Criminal Justice Act 1948 (towards the cost of probation services) and under section 27 of the Justices of the Peace Act 1949 (grants for magistrates' courts purposes), and

(*b*) under section 31 of the Police Act 1964 (police grants), whether made to a committee of a local authority or not,

shall be treated for the purposes of subsection (2) above as grants made to local authorities; and to the extent that, in any year, any expenditure of the Receiver for the Metropolitan Police District or of a combined police authority is met by any such grants, that expenditure shall be treated for the purposes of this section as relevant expenditure in relation to that year.

(7) In this section—

"housing subsidies" means such grants to local authorities out of money provided by Parliament for housing as may be determined by the Secretary of State to be housing subsidies for the purposes of this section; and

"rate fund", in relation to the Greater London Council, the Common Council of the City of London and the Council of the Isles of Scilly, means the general fund or general rate, as the case may require, and in relation to any other local authority means the county fund or general rate fund.

(8) The provisions of Part I of Schedule 1 to this Act shall have effect with respect to the termination of grants under section 1 of the Local Government Act 1966 (existing rate support grants). [**201**]

GENERAL NOTE TO PART I

"Prescribed" means prescribed by a rate support grant order (s. 10 (2)).

For the meaning of local authorities, see s. 10 (1).

"Year" means a period of twelve months beginning with 1st April (s. 10 (1)).

"Regulations." Throughout this Part, the Secretary of State is given powers to make regulations. The exercise of any such power is by way of statutory instrument Before making any such regulations the Secretary of State must consult with such associations of local authorities as appear to him to be concerned and with any local authority with whom consultation appears to him to be desirable—s. 10 (5). All such regulations are subject to the negative Parliamentary procedure—s. 10 (4). (Contrast the rate support grant order—s. 3 (2)). For statutory instruments and the negative procedure, see Statutory Instruments Act 1946, ss. 1 and 5.

EXPLANATORY NOTE

See paras. [**1**]–[**6**], *ante*.

DEFINITIONS

"Relevant expenditure." See s. 1 (4).

"Amount available for grants." This is the aggregate amount which the Secretary of State estimates is to be available for the payment out of money provided by Parliament of grants (other than housing subsidies and under s. 8 below), to local authorities in respect of their relevant expenditure—s. 1 (2).

"Estimated aggregate amount of the rate support grants." This is the amount available for grant less certain items—s. 1 (2) (*a*), (*b*), (*c*).

"Consult." This imposes a duty not only to receive and bona fide consider any relevant facts and opinions put forward by those entitled to be consulted, but also to postively seek out the views of those concerned, to give them sufficient information to enable them to tender advice, and sufficient opportunity to do so. See *Fletcher* v. *Minister of Town and Country Planning*, [1947] 2 All E.R. 496; *Rollo* v. *Minister of Town and Country Planning*, [1948] 1 All E.R.; *Port Louis Corp.* v. *A.G. of Mauritius*, [1965] A.C. 111; *Re Union of the Benefices of Whippingham and East Cowes*, [1954] 2 All E.R. 22; *Agricultural Industry Training Board* v. *Aylesbury Mushrooms, Ltd.*, [1972] 1 All E.R. 280.

SUB-S. (8)

Note that Sch. 1, Part I, *post*, deals with the method of increasing during 1974–75 the amount of rate support grant for the year 1973–74.

2. Elements of rate support grants

(1) The aggregate amount of the rate support grants for any year shall be divided by the Secretary of State into three elements, to be known respectively as "the needs element", "the domestic element" and "the resources element", and the aggregate amount of the needs element and of the domestic element and the estimated aggregate amount of the resources element shall be such as may be prescribed.

(2) Subject to the following provisions of this section, payments in respect of the elements of rate support grant shall be made to a local authority at such times as the Secretary of State may with the consent of the Treasury determine, and shall be made in aid of the revenues of the authority generally; and the provisions of Schedule 2 to this Act shall have effect with respect to the determination of the amounts payable to any local authority in respect of those elements for any year.

(3) Except as provided by subsection (4) below, no payment in respect of the needs element shall be made to the council of a non-metropolitan district and the Secretary of State may by regulations provide that such proportion as may be determined by or under the regulations of the amount which, apart from the regulations, would be payable in respect of the needs element for any year—

(*a*) to the council of a London borough or the Common Council of the City of London, or

(*b*) to the council of a metropolitan district,

shall be payable instead to the Greater London Council or, as the case may be, to the council of the metropolitan county in which the district is situated; and any such regulations may make different provision in relation to different councils.

(4) The Secretary of State may by regulations provide that such proportion as may be determined by or under the regulations of the amount which, apart from the regulations, would be payable in respect of the needs element for any year to the council of a non-metropolitan county shall, in such cases as may be determined in accordance with the regulations, be payable instead to the councils of districts situated in the county; and any such regulations may make different provision in relation to different councils.

(5) No payment in respect of either the domestic element or the resources element shall be made to a county council or the Greater London Council.

(6) Any amounts payable to a local authority in respect of the domestic element shall be taken into account for the purposes of this and any other Act as if they were payable on account of rates.

(7) Subject to subsection (8) below, the Secretary of State may—

(*a*) defray any expenditure incurred in any year in the provision of services for local authorities by any body specified in regulations made by the Secretary of State; and

(*b*) deduct from the aggregate amount of the needs element for that year such amount, not exceeding the total of the expenditure so defrayed, as appears to him to be appropriate.

(8) Before exercising his powers under subsection (7) above, the Secretary of State shall consult with such associations of local authorities as appear to him to be concerned and with any local authority with whom consultation appears to him to be desirable. [**202**]

EXPLANATORY NOTE

See paras. [**7**]–[**18**], *ante*.

DEFINITIONS

"Prescribed." This means prescribed by a rate support grant order.
"Regulations." See General Note to Part I, *ante*.
"Consult." See definition in notes to s. 1, *ante*.

REGULATIONS

See the Rate Support Grant (Specified Bodies) Regulations 1974 S.I. 1974 No. 788 made under sub. (7) (*a*) above.

3. Rate support grant orders

(1) The estimated aggregate amount of the rate support grants fixed in accordance with section 1 (2) above for any year and the matters which under this Part of this Act are to be prescribed shall be fixed and prescribed by an order (in this Part of this Act referred to as a "rate support grant order") made by the Secretary of State with the consent of the Treasury and after consultation with such associations of local authorities as appear to the Secretary of State to be concerned and with any local authority with whom consultation appears to him to be desirable.

(2) Every rate support grant order shall be laid before the Commons House of Parliament and shall not have effect until approved by a resolution of that House.

(3) Together with any rate support grant order laid before the Commons House of Parliament there shall be laid a report of the considerations leading to the provisions of the order, including the considerations leading to the determination of the amount available for grants and the portions mentioned in paragraphs (*a*) to (*c*) of section 1 (2) above.

(4) A separate rate support grant order shall be made in advance for each year. [**203**]

DEFINITION

"Estimated aggregate amount of the rate support grants." See note to s. 1, *ante*.

Sub-s. (4). Note that in contrast with the Local Government Act 1966, a rate support grant order is made for one year only.

ORDER

See the Rate Support Grant Order 1974, S.I. 1974 No. 550.

4. Variation of rate support grant orders

(1) If it appears to the Secretary of State that, after the time when the amount available for grants was determined for any year, the relevant expenditure of local authorities for that year has been or is likely to be substantially increased by reason of—

(*a*) an increase which has taken place in the level of prices, costs or remuneration, or

(*b*) the coming into operation of a provision of an enactment passed after this Act,

and that no account was taken of that increase or, as the case may be, the effect of that provision when the amount available for grants was so determined, he may for that year redetermine that amount and the portions which are to be deducted therefrom in accordance with section 1 (2) above and, by an order made in the like manner and subject to the like provisions as a rate support grant order, may increase the amounts fixed by the relevant rate support grant order as the estimated aggregate amount of the rate support grants and the aggregate amount of the needs element for that year.

(2) The provisions of sections 1 (3) and 3 (3) above relating to consultation and to a report of the considerations leading to a determination under section 1 above shall apply to a redetermination under this section as they apply to a determination under that section.

(3) In redetermining under this section the amount available for grants and the portions referred to in subsection (1) above, the Secretary of State—

(*a*) shall take into account not only the effect of the increase referred to in paragraph (*a*) of that subsection or, as the case may be, the provision referred to in paragraph (*b*) thereof, but also any future variation in the level of prices, costs and remuneration current at the time of the redetermination which in his opinion will result from any such decisions as are referred to in section 1 (3) (*d*) above, and

(*b*) except in the case of a change resulting from the coming into operation of any enactment passed after this Act, shall take no account of any change, as compared with the situation at the time that amount and those portions were determined for the purposes of the relevant rate support grant order, in the demand for services giving rise to relevant expenditure, in the need for developing those services, in the extent to which those services have been developed or in the extent to which having regard to general economic conditions, it is reasonable to develop those services.

(4) An order made under subsection (1) above in respect of any year shall specify the actual (and not the estimated) aggregate amount of the resources element for that year.

(5) If, in a case where the Secretary of State proposes to make an order under subsection (1) above in respect of any year, it appears to him that, apart from any provision made by virtue of this subsection, the effect of the order and of any other order under subsection (1) above which he considers likely to be made in respect of that year would be that the ratio between the actual aggregate amount of the resources element for that year and the aggregate amount of the needs element for that year would be significantly different from the ratio (in this subsection referred to as "the expected ratio") between the estimated aggregate amount of the resources element for that year, as fixed by the relevant rate support grant order, and the aggregate amount of the needs element, as so fixed, he may in the order under subsection (1) above—

(*a*) specify as the aggregate amount of the resources element for that year such amount as, in his estimation, will secure that (taking account of the effect of any further orders likely to be made under subsection (1) above in respect of that year) the ratio which the amount so specified will bear to the aggregate amount of the needs element for that year will be the expected ratio; and

(*b*) in order to secure that the total amount paid in respect of the resources element to local authorities entitled to payments in respect of that element does not exceed the amount specified as mentioned in paragraph (*a*) above, make provision for a corresponding variation in the amount payable to each such authority in respect of that element.

(6) Except as provided by the preceding provisions of this section, an order under subsection (1) above in respect of any year shall not vary the amount of the elements of the rate support grants for that year but, subject thereto, any such order may, as respects the year to which it relates, vary any matters prescribed by the relevant rate support grant order other than—

(*a*) the additional factors prescribed by that order for the purposes of paragraph 1 of Schedule 2 to this Act; and

(*b*) any matter prescribed by that order in relation to the domestic element or the resources element.

(7) In this section "relevant expenditure" has the same meaning as in section 1 above. [**204**]

EXPLANATORY NOTE

See paras. [**19**]–[**21**], *ante*.

DEFINITIONS

"Relevant expenditure." See s. 1 (4).
"Amount available for grants." See note to s. 1, *ante*.
"Estimated aggregate amount of the rate support grants." See note to s. 1, *ante*.

5. Reduction of grants in case of default

(1) If, in the case of any local authority or joint board, the appropriate Minister—

(*a*) is satisfied that the authority or board have failed to achieve or maintain a reasonable standard in the discharge of any of their functions, regard being had to the standards maintained by other authorities and boards, and

(*b*) is of opinion that by reason of the failure a reduction should be made in the amount of any elements of rate support grant payable to the local authority or a constituent authority of the joint board,

he may, after affording to the local or constituent authority in question an opportunity of making representations, make and cause to be laid before Parliament a report stating the amount of and the reasons for the proposed reduction and setting out any representations made by the authority with respect to the proposed reduction; and if the report is approved by a resolution of the Commons House of Parliament the Secretary of State may reduce the elements of the grant accordingly.

(2) The appropriate Minister may make regulations for prescribing standards and general requirements in relation to any function of a local authority; and in determining for the purposes of subsection (1) above whether there has been such a failure as is mentioned in that subsection, regard shall be had to any such regulations and any other standards or requirements imposed by or under any enactment.

(3) Any regulations in force immediately before 1st April 1974 and—

(*a*) made under subsection (2) of section 4 of the Local Government Act 1966 (which in the context of that Act corresponds to subsection (2) above), or

(*b*) made under section 3 (4) of the Local Government Act 1958 but, by virtue of subsection (3) of the said section 4, having effect for the purposes of that section as if made under subsection (2) thereof,

shall have effect on and after that date for the purposes of this section as if made under subsection (2) above.

(4) In this section "joint board" includes a joint committee which continues to exist by virtue of section 263 (5) of the Local Government Act 1972. **[205]**

EXPLANATORY NOTE

See paras. [**22**]–[**25**], *ante*.

DEFINITIONS

"Local authority." See s. 10 (1).

"Joint board." Note sub-s. (4) above. S. 263 (5) of the Local Government Act 1972 continues the existence of certain joint committees exercising functions for an area which on 1st April 1974 lies within the area of two or more new local authorities.

"Regulations". See General Note to Part I, *ante*.

SUB-S. (3)

Regulations made under s. 4 (2) of the Local Government Act 1966 are the Training of Teachers Regulations 1967, S.I. 1967 No. 792, amended by S.I. 1969 No. 848.

Regulations made under s. 3 (4) of the Local Government Act 1958 are the Schools Regulations 1959, S.I. 1959 No. 364, amended by S.I. 1963 No. 1468, S.I. 1964 No. 1311, S.I. 1965 No. 3, S.I. 1966 No. 1577, S.I. 1968 No. 1281, S.I. 1969 Nos. 231, 1174, 1777, S.I. 1971 No. 342, S.I. 1973 No. 2021; the Further Education Regulations 1969, S.I. 1969 No. 403, as amended by S.I. 1970 No. 586; the Training of Teachers Regulations 1967, S.I. 1967, No. 792, amended by S.I. 1969 No. 848; the Handicapped Pupils (Boarding) Regulations 1959, S.I. 1959 No. 362; and the Qualified Teachers and Teachers in Special Schools Regulations, S.I. 1971 No. 342.

Grants for particular purposes

6. Supplementary grants for transport purposes

(1) For the year 1975–76 and each subsequent year the Secretary of State shall make, in accordance with the provisions of this section, supplementary grants (in this section referred to as "supplementary grants for transport purposes") to county councils and the Greater London Council in respect of their estimated expenditure in connection with—

(*a*) public transport,

(*b*) highways,

(*c*) the regulation of traffic, and

(*d*) the provision of parking places,

and the matters specified in paragraphs (*a*) to (*d*) above are in this section referred to as "transport matters".

(2) To the extent that it would not otherwise be so included, there shall be treated for the purposes of this section as included in a council's estimated expenditure in connection with transport matters their estimated capital expenditure in connection with the provision by any person of facilities for or in connection with the loading or unloading of freight carried or intended to be carried otherwise than by road.

(3) The aggregate amount of supplementary grants for transport purposes for any year shall be such as may be prescribed.

(4) The proportion of the aggregate amount of supplementary grants for transport purposes payable for any year to a county council or the Greater London Council shall be determined, by such method as may be prescribed for the purposes of this section, by reference to the extent (if any) to which the accepted estimated expenditure of the council for the year in connection with transport matters exceeds a level of expenditure determined in such manner and by reference to such factors as may be prescribed for the purposes of this section.

(5) For the purposes of subsection (4) above,—

(*a*) the Secretary of State may treat the estimated expenditure of the London borough councils and the Common Council of the City of London in connection with transport matters as forming part of the estimated expenditure in connection with those matters of the Greater London Council;

(*b*) the Secretary of State may treat the estimated expenditure of a district council in connection with transport matters as forming part of the estimated expenditure in connection with those matters of the council of the county in which the district is situated; and

(*c*) "accepted", in relation to the estimated expenditure of a council, means so much of their estimated expenditure as the Secretary of State may determine to be appropriate to be taken into account for the purposes of this section;

and in making a determination under paragraph (*c*) above, in relation to the estimated expenditure of a council, the Secretary of State shall have regard to the progress which appears to him to have been made by the council in formulating and implementing suitable policies to meet the needs of their area in connection with transport matters.

(6) Payments of supplementary grants for transport purposes shall be made at such times as the Secretary of State may, with the consent of the Treasury, determine.

(7) The Secretary of State may by regulations make such supplementary provision as he considers appropriate in relation to any factor prescribed for the purposes of this section in accordance with subsection (4) above.

(8) In consequence of the introduction of supplementary grants for transport purposes and of the provisions of this Part of this Act relating to rate support grants, the provisions of Part II of Schedule 1 to this Act shall have effect with respect to certain grants under the Highways Act 1959 and the Transport Act 1968. [**206**]

EXPLANATORY NOTE

See paras. [**26**]–[**31**], *ante*.

DEFINITIONS

"Prescribed" means prescribed by a rate support grant order.

"Regulations." See General Note to Part I, *ante*.

7. Supplementary grants towards expenditure with respect to National Parks

(1) For the year 1974–75 and each subsequent year the Secretary of State shall make, in accordance with the provisions of this section, supplementary grants to county councils in respect of their estimated expenditure in connection with National Parks.

(2) The aggregate amount of supplementary grants under this section for any year shall be such as may be prescribed.

(3) Supplementary grants under this section shall be payable only to county councils whose areas include the whole or any part of a National Park, and the proportion of the aggregate amount of supplementary grants under this section payable for any year to a county council shall be determined, by such method as may be prescribed for the purposes of this section, by reference to so much of the estimated expenditure of the council with respect to National Parks as the Secretary of State, after consultation with the Countryside Commission, may determine to be appropriate to be taken into account for the purposes of this section.

(4) Payments of supplementary grants under this section shall be made at such times as the Secretary of State may, with the consent of the Treasury, determine. [**207**]

EXPLANATORY NOTE

See paras. [**32**]–[**35**], *ante*.

DEFINITIONS

"Prescribed" means prescribed by a rate support grant order. For provisions under this section for the year 1974–75, see the Rate Support Grant Order 1974, S.I. 1974 No. 550, art. 4.

"National Park." See National Parks and Access to the Countryside Act 1949, s. 5.

"Countryside Commission." See Countryside Act 1968, s. 1.

8. Specific grants for purposes not covered by rate support grants

(1) For the year 1974–75 and each subsequent year, the Secretary of State shall pay—

(*a*) to any rating authority granting rebates under the statutory rate rebate scheme in that year a grant equal to 90 per cent. of the aggregate amount of the rebates so granted; and

(*b*) to any rating authority granting rebates under a local rate rebate scheme in that year a grant equal to 90 per cent. of the aggregate amount of the rebates which, if that scheme had not been in force, would have been granted under the statutory rate rebate scheme during that year or, as the case may require, during the part of the year when the local rate rebate scheme was in force.

(2) For the year 1974–75 and each subsequent year the Secretary of State shall pay to each local education authority a grant equal to 90 per cent. of the aggregate amount paid in that year by the authority—

(*a*) in pursuance of awards bestowed under section 1 (1) of the Education Act 1962 (for persons attending first degree university courses and comparable courses); and

(*b*) by way of grants under section 2 (3) of that Act (to or in respect of persons undergoing training as teachers).

(3) Payments of grants under subsection (1) or subsection (2) above shall be made at such times as the Secretary of State may, with the consent of the Treasury, determine.

(4) In subsection (1) above "the statutory rate rebate scheme" and "local rate rebate scheme" have the same meanings as in Part II of this Act.

(5) The provisions of Part III of Schedule 1 to this Act shall have effect with respect to the termination of certain grants for specific purposes, other than highways and public transport. [**208**]

EXPLANATORY NOTE

See para. [**36**], *ante*.

DEFINITIONS

"Statutory rate rebate scheme." See s. 11, *post*.
"Local rate rebate scheme." See s. 12, *post*.

9. Grants and loans by the Countryside Commission

(1) In accordance with arrangements approved by the Secretary of State and the Treasury, the Countryside Commission may give financial assistance by way of grant or loan, or partly in the one way and partly in the other, to any person in respect of expenditure incurred by him in doing anything which, in the opinion of the Commission, is conducive to the attainment of any of the purposes of the Countryside Act 1968 or the National Parks and Access to the Countryside Act 1949.

(2) On making a grant or loan under this section the Countryside Commission may impose such conditions as they think fit including (in the case of a grant) conditions for repayment in specified circumstances.

(3) The exercise of the Countryside Commission's power under this section shall be subject to any directions given to the Commission by the Secretary of State.

(4) The provisions of this section shall have effect in place of the provisions of section 5 of the Countryside Act 1968 (under which grants may be made only to persons other than public bodies and only in respect of projects approved by the Secretary of State). [**209**]

EXPLANATORY NOTE

See paras. [**37**]–[**39**], *ante*.

DEFINITION

"Any person." This includes a private person as well as a public body (see sub-s. (4) above).

SUB-S. (1)

The purposes of the Acts in question include the conservation and enhancement of natural beauty, the maintenance of nature reserves, and of public paths, the securing of access to the open countryside and the provision of opportunities for the enjoyment of the countryside by the public.

SUB-S. (2)

"Such conditions as they think fit." For judicial control of the validity of conditions see, *e.g.*, *Mixnam's Properties Ltd.* v. *Chertsey U.D.C.*, [1965] A.C. 735.

Supplementary

10. Supplementary provisions for Part I

(1) The following bodies are local authorities for the purposes of this Part of this Act, namely—

(*a*) the council of a county,
(*b*) the Greater London Council,
(*c*) the council of a district,
(*d*) the council of a London borough,
(*e*) the Common Council of the City of London, and
(*f*) the Council of the Isles of Scilly,

and for the purposes of the provisions of this Act relating to the domestic element the Sub-Treasurer of the Inner Temple and the Under Treasurer of the Middle Temple shall also be local authorities.

(2) In this Part of this Act—

"the amount available for grants" has the meaning assigned to it by section 1 (2) above;
"the appropriate Minister" means, in relation to any matter, the Minister in charge of the Government department concerned or primarily concerned with that matter;
"the domestic element", "the needs element" and "the resources element" shall be construed in accordance with section 2 (1) above;
"prescribed" means prescribed by a rate support grant order; and
"year" means a period of twelve months beginning with 1st April.

(3) The Secretary of State may make regulations for carrying the provisions of sections 1 to 5 of and Schedule 2 to this Act into effect and, without prejudice to the generality of this provision,—

(*a*) for determining the manner in which any calculation or estimate is to be made for any of the purposes of those provisions;
(*b*) for determining the authority or person by or to whom any information required for those purposes is to be given and the time at which and the form in which it is to be given;
(*c*) for providing that the calculations or estimates by reference to which any payments are made may be treated as either conclusive or provisional or conclusive for some purposes and provisional for other purposes and, in so far as they are treated as provisional, for the making of further calculations or estimates based on information not previously available and for adjusting, in the light thereof, any payment already made;

and regulations under this subsection may make different provisions for different circumstances.

(4) Any power conferred by any provision of this Part of this Act to make regulations shall be exercisable by statutory instrument, which shall be subject to annulment in pursuance of a resolution of either House of Parliament.

(5) Before making regulations under any provision of this Part of this Act, the Secretary of State shall consult with such associations of local authorities as appear to him to be concerned and with any local authority with whom consultation appears to him to be desirable. [**210**]

DEFINITION

"Statutory instrument." See Statutory Instruments Act 1946.

REGULATIONS

The Rate Support Grant Regulations 1974, S.I. 1974 No. 428.

Part II

Rating

11. The statutory rate rebate scheme

(1) The Secretary of State shall by regulations make, with the consent of the Treasury, a scheme (in this Part of this Act referred to as "the statutory rate rebate scheme") for the grant by rating authorities to residential occupiers of rebates from rates calculated in accordance with the provisions of the scheme by reference to their needs and their resources.

(2) The statutory rate rebate scheme shall have effect in respect of rebate periods beginning on or after 1st April 1974, and accordingly no person shall be entitled in respect of any such rebate period to a rate rebate under section 49 of the principal Act.

(3) Without prejudice to the generality of the power conferred by sub-section (1) above, the statutory rate rebate scheme may contain provisions corresponding, so far as the Secretary of State considers appropriate, to provisions of Part I of Schedule 3 or Part I of Schedule 4 to the Housing Finance Act 1972 (model schemes of rent rebates and rent allowances).

(4) In this Part of this Act "rebate period" means such period as may be determined in accordance with the statutory rate rebate scheme, and that scheme may make provision for the determination of different periods in relation to different residential occupiers or different classes of residential occupiers. [**211**]

GENERAL NOTE TO PART II

Expressions used in this Part of this Act have the same meaning as in the General Rate Act 1967 except in so far as otherwise provided.

EXPLANATORY NOTE

See paras. [**42**]–[**44**], *ante*.

DEFINITIONS

"Regulations." These are to be made by statutory instrument—s. 22 (3) of this Act, and s. 114 of the General Rate Act 1967.

"Rating authorities." See General Rate Act 1967, s. 1, Local Government Act 1972, Sch. 13, para. 28

"Residential occupier." See s. 13 (1).

"Rebate period." As defined in sub-s. (4) above, not in the General Rate Act 1967.

REGULATIONS

The Rate Rebate Regulations 1974, S.I. 1974 No. 411.

12. Local rate rebate schemes

(1) Subject to the following provisions of this section, a rating authority may by resolution make for their area a scheme (in this Part of this Act referred to as a "local rate rebate scheme") for the grant by the authority to residential occupiers of rebates from rates calculated in accordance with the provisions of the scheme by reference to their needs and resources.

(2) A local rate rebate scheme may take the form of a scheme distinct from the statutory rate rebate scheme or may operate by way of variation of that scheme, and accordingly any reference in this Part of this Act to a local rate rebate scheme includes a reference to the statutory rate rebate scheme as so varied.

(3) A local rate rebate scheme shall be so framed as to secure that, in the estimate of the rating authority—

(*a*) for any rebate period no person will be entitled under the scheme to a rate rebate less than that to which he would be entitled under the statutory rate rebate scheme; and

(*b*) the total of the rebates which will be allowable under the local rate rebate scheme in any year will not exceed the permitted total of rebates for that year.

(4) In relation to a local rate rebate scheme for any area, the permitted total of rebates for any year is 110 per cent. of the total of the rate rebates which (if the local rate rebate scheme had not been in force) would have been allowable in that year to residential occupiers in that area under the statutory rate rebate scheme.

(5) A local rate rebate scheme may be revoked or varied by a further resolution of the rating authority and, except in so far as the Secretary of State otherwise directs—

(*a*) any such scheme and any variation thereof shall take effect with respect to any rebate period beginning on or after such date as may be specified in the rating authority's resolution, and

(*b*) a resolution revoking a local rate rebate scheme shall take effect at the expiry of any rebate period which is current, or which expires, on such date as may be specified in the resolution,

and, as soon as practicable after a rating authority has passed a resolution making, varying or revoking a local rate rebate scheme, the authority shall send a copy of the resolution to the Secretary of State.

(6) As soon as practicable after the end of any year in which a local rate rebate scheme has been in operation, and in any case not later than 31st July next following, the rating authority concerned shall send to the Secretary of State a certificate specifying—

(*a*) the total amount of the rate rebates allowed in that year under the local rate rebate scheme, and

(*b*) the permitted total of rebates for that year and, if the local rate rebate scheme was not in operation during the whole of that year, the fraction of that permitted total which corresponds to the fraction of the year during which the local scheme was in operation.

(7) Where it appears from a certificate under subsection (6) above that the amount specified as mentioned in paragraph (*a*) of that subsection exceeds the permitted total or, as the case may be, the appropriate fraction of the permitted total referred to in paragraph (*b*) of that subsection, it shall be the duty of the rating authority to send to the Secretary of State, together with that certificate, a statement of—

(*a*) their proposals for varying or revoking the local rate rebate scheme so as to secure that the total of the rate rebates allowed in the year following that to which the certificate relates will not exceed the permitted total of rebates for that year; or

(*b*) their reasons for believing that no change is necessary in the local rate rebate scheme in order to secure that result.

(8) If the Secretary of State is of the opinion that any proposals made by a rating authority under subsection (7) (*a*) above will not secure the result referred to in that subsection, or that some variation of a local rate rebate scheme

will be required to secure that result, notwithstanding the contrary view expressed by a rating authority in a statement under subsection (7) (*b*) above, or if it comes to the knowledge of the Secretary of State that the condition in subsection (3) (*a*) above is not fulfilled with respect to the entitlement of any person to a rate rebate under a local rate rebate scheme, the Secretary of State may by order provide—

(*a*) that from such date as may be specified in the order the local rate rebate scheme shall have effect subject to such variations as may be so specified and that, within such minimum period as may be specified, no other variations may be made in the scheme by the rating authority; or

(*b*) that the local rate rebate scheme shall be revoked with effect from such date as may be specified in the order and that no new local rate rebate scheme shall be brought into operation for the rating area concerned within such period as may be so specified. [**212**]

EXPLANATORY NOTE

See paras. [**45**]–[**49**], *ante*.

DEFINITIONS

"Rating Authority." See note to s. 11, *ante*.
"Residential occupier." See s. 13 (1).
"Rebate period." See s. 11 (4).
"Permitted total of rebates." See s. 12 (4).
"By order." This, under s. 12 (8), will be by statutory instrument (see s. 22 (3)).

13. Residential occupiers

(1) Subject to subsections (2) and (3) below, the following persons are residential occupiers for the purposes of this Part of this Act, namely—

(*a*) a person who is the occupier of, and resides or is usually resident in, a hereditament which is a dwelling-house and which at the relevant date has a rateable value not exceeding the specified limit;

(*b*) a person who is the occupier of a hereditament which is not a dwelling-house, but who resides or is usually resident in a part of the hereditament which is used for the purposes of a private dwelling and has at the relevant date a rateable value not exceeding the specified limit;

(*c*) a person who, not being the occupier of any such hereditament as is mentioned in paragraph (*a*) or paragraph (*b*) above, resides or is usually resident in a part of any such hereditament, which part is used for the purposes of a private dwelling and at the relevant date has a rateable value not exceeding the specified limit, and in respect of which he makes payments by way of rent to the occupier or any other person who is himself a residential occupier.

(2) Where two or more persons are joint occupiers of a hereditament such as is mentioned in paragraph (*a*) or paragraph (*b*) of subsection (1) above, or joint tenants of such a part thereof as is mentioned in paragraph (*c*) of that subsection, then, for the purposes of rate rebates under the statutory rate rebate scheme or a local rate rebate scheme, the rating authority may treat one of those persons as if he were the sole occupier of the hereditament or, as the case may be, sole tenant or that part thereof.

(3) For the purposes of paragraphs (*b*) and (*c*) of subsection (1) above, the rateable value on any day of part of a hereditament shall be taken to be such

value as is found by a proper apportionment of the rateable value of the whole hereditament on that day; and any question arising under this subsection as to the proper apportionment of any rateable value shall be determined by the county court, whose decision shall be final.

(4) In subsection (1) above—

(*a*) "the relevant date", in relation to a person making an application for a rate rebate under the statutory rate rebate scheme or a local rate rebate scheme, means the beginning of the year in any part of which a rebate granted to him in pursuance of the application will be effective, and

(*b*) "the specified limit", in relation to a hereditament, means such limit of rateable value as the Secretary of State may by order specify for the purposes of this section in relation to hereditaments in the rating area in which that hereditament is situated. [**213**]

EXPLANATORY NOTE

See paras. [**50**]–[**53**], *ante*.

SPECIFIED LIMIT

The Rate Rebates (Limits of Rateable Value) Order 1974, S.I. 1974 No. 412, made under sub-s. (4) (*b*) above, specifies limits of £1,500 in Greater London and £750 elsewhere.

DEFINITIONS

"Hereditament." See General Rates Act 1967, s. 115.
"Dwelling-house." See General Rate Act 1967, s. 115.
"Statutory rate rebate scheme." See s. 11.
"Local rate rebate scheme." See s. 12.

14. Supplementary provisions as to eligibility for rate rebates

(1) Subject to subsection (2) below, no residential occupier liable for rates in respect of a hereditament in any area shall be eligible to apply for a rate rebate under the statutory rate rebate scheme in respect of those rates for any rebate period during which a local rate rebate scheme is in operation in that area.

(2) If any such residential occupier as is referred to in subsection (1) above shows to the satisfaction of the rating authority that the local rate rebate scheme does not in his case fulfil the condition in section 12 (3) (*a*) above, he shall be eligible to apply for a rate rebate under the statutory rate rebate scheme and, if he makes such an application for any rebate period, he shall cease to be eligible to make an application for that period under the local rate rebate scheme.

(3) If, in a case where a residential occupier is liable for rates in respect of a hereditament for a rate period beginning on or after 1st April 1974,—

(*a*) the residential occupier is entitled to a rebate from those rates under the statutory rate rebate scheme or a local rate rebate scheme, and

(*b*) the rating authority affords him relief in respect of those rates under section 53 of the principal Act (reduction or remission of payment of rates on account of poverty),

the rating authority shall grant him a rebate as mentioned in paragraph (*a*) above only if, and to the extent that, the amount of the rebate exceeds the aggregate amount afforded him as mentioned in paragraph (*b*) above.

(4) In section 16 (2) of the Ministry of Social Security Act 1966 (rate rebates

to which persons in receipt of supplementary benefit might otherwise be entitled reduced if their requirements were determined without regard to any rate rebate) for the words "section 5 of the Rating Act 1966" there shall be substituted the words "a scheme under section 11 or section 12 of the Local Government Act 1974". [**214**]

EXPLANATORY NOTE

See paras. [**51**]–[**53**], *ante*.

DEFINITIONS

"Residential occupier." See s. 13 (1).
"Statutory rate rebate scheme." See s. 11.
"Local rate rebate scheme." See s. 12.
"Rating authority." See note to s. 11, *ante*.

15. Rating of unoccupied property

(1) In section 17 of the principal Act (rating of unoccupied property in accordance with Schedule 1 to that Act) in subsection (2)—

(*a*) so much of paragraph (*a*) as provides that, except with the authority of the Secretary of State, a resolution providing that the provisions of Schedule 1 to that Act shall apply to an area may not take effect within the period of seven years beginning with the day on which those provisions ceased or last ceased to apply to that area, and

(*b*) so much of paragraph (*b*) as provides that, except with the authority of the Secretary of State, a resolution providing that the provisions of Schedule 1 to that Act shall cease to apply to an area may not take effect within the period of seven years beginning with the day on which those provisions came or last came into operation in that area,

shall cease to have effect.

(2) In subsection (5) of that section for the words "This section and the said Schedule 1 shall not apply to the Temples, and in their application" there shall be substituted the words "In the application of this section and the said Schedule 1".

(3) In paragraph 1 (1) of Schedule 1 to the principal Act (where, by virtue of a resolution under section 17 of that Act, that Schedule is in operation in any area, every relevant hereditament in that area which is unoccupied for a continuous period exceeding three months shall be rated in accordance with the provisions of that Schedule) after the words "in that area" there shall be inserted the words "or, if only a class or classes of relevant hereditament is or are for the time being specified by a resolution of the rating authority for the purposes of this paragraph, any relevant hereditament in that area which falls within that class or any of those classes".

(4) In sub-paragraph (2) of paragraph 1 of Schedule 1 to the principal Act (the amount of rates payable in respect of a vacant hereditament to be one-half of the amount which would be payable if the hereditament were occupied) for the words "one-half" there shall be substituted the words "the specified proportion", and at the end of that sub-paragraph there shall be inserted the following sub-paragraph—

"(2A) In sub-paragraph (2) above 'the specified proportion', in relation to a hereditament, means such proportion (which may be the whole or any less amount) as may be specified for the purposes of this sub-paragraph by a resolution of the rating authority for the rating area in which the hereditament is situated; and different proportions may be so specified in relation to different classes of hereditaments and in relation to hereditaments in different parts of the rating area."

(5) After paragraph 3 of Schedule 1 to the principal Act there shall be inserted the following paragraph—

"3A. Without prejudice to section 53 of this Act, a rating authority shall have power to reduce or remit the payment of any rates payable in respect of a hereditament by virtue of paragraph 1 of this Schedule if they consider that the payment would cause hardship to the person liable for those rates."

(6) At the end of paragraph 14 of Schedule 1 to the principal Act there shall be added the following sub-paragraph—

"(2) In calculating any period for the purposes of this Schedule in relation to a hereditament which is of a class specified by the rating authority for the purposes of paragraph 1 above, any earlier period during which classes of relevant hereditament were, but no class comprising that hereditament was, so specified shall be disregarded." [**215**]

EXPLANATORY NOTE

See paras. [**54**]–[**59**], *ante*.

DEFINITION

"Principal Act." This is the General Rate Act 1967.

16. Rating surcharge on unused office, etc., property

The following sections shall be inserted after section 17 of the principal Act—

"17A. Liability to progressive surcharge in respect of unused office, etc., property

(1) If for a continuous period exceeding six months a commercial building is not used for the purpose for which it was constructed or has been adapted, its owner shall pay in respect of that period (the 'period of non-use') a surcharge additional to the rates (if any) payable apart from this section.

(2) Subsection (1) of this section shall not apply where—

(*a*) the owner has tried his best to let the building, or
(*b*) the condition of the building makes it unfit for use for the purpose for which it was constructed or has been adapted, and it cannot be rendered fit at a cost which is reasonable in relation to the value of that use.

(3) Where the owner is in occupation of the building throughout the period of non-use, the surcharge shall be levied in the form of rates by doubling the normal rates for the first twelve months of the period of non-use, trebling the normal rates for the second twelve months, quadrupling the normal rates for the third twelve months, and so on progressively while the period of non-use lasts.

In this subsection 'the normal rates', in relation to any period, means the rates payable in respect of that period apart from this section (taking rates as accruing uniformly from day to day); and where the period of non-use extends through part only of any twelve-month period, the surcharge shall be calculated by reference to the normal rates for that part.

(4) Where the owner is not in occupation of the building throughout the period of non-use—

(*a*) the amount of the surcharge shall be the same as it would have been if the owner had been in occupation of the building throughout the period of non-use, and

(*b*) the surcharge shall be levied in the form of rates of that amount as if they were payable by the owner in respect of that occupation.

(5) In determining whether or not the owner has tried his best to let the building, regard shall be had to the following, as well as other relevant factors—

(*a*) the rent sought, compared with rents of similar properties in the area,

(*b*) the other covenants and conditions required by the owner to be contained in any proposed lease,

(*c*) whether or not the owner indicated to prospective lessees that he was prepared to let the building in parts,

(*d*) the number and resources of the firms of estate agents retained for the purpose of letting the building, and

(*e*) the nature and extent of advertising of the building by the owner or those agents.

17B. Supplemental provisions as to section 17A

(1) A rating authority may serve a notice on the owner of any commercial building requiring him to make a written return containing such particulars as may be reasonably required by the authority for the purposes of section 17A of this Act; and subsections (3) to (6) of section 82 of this Act shall apply to a notice under this subsection as they apply to a notice under section 82, as if—

(*a*) the reference in section 82 (3) to the valuation officer were a reference to the rating authority, and

(*b*) the penalties laid down by section 82 (4) and (5) were—

(i) on summary conviction, a fine not exceeding £400; and

(ii) on conviction on indictment, imprisonment for a term not exceeding two years, or a fine, or both.

(2) References in section 17A of this Act and this section to a commercial building are references to a hereditament (not being a dwelling-house, or a hereditament having a floor space not exceeding 240 square feet and used as a lock-up garage) whose net annual value falls to be ascertained under section 19 (2) of this Act; and if during a period of non-use a commercial building is divided into two or more hereditaments, the amount of any surcharge imposed under section 17A of this Act in respect of any of those hereditaments shall be the same as if it had been a separate hereditament from the beginning of the period of non-use.

(3) A surcharge imposed under section 17A of this Act in respect of a hereditament shall until recovered be a charge on the land comprised in the hereditament; and for the purposes of the application to such a charge

of section 15 (registration of local land charges) of the Land Charges Act 1925 this Act shall be deemed to be a similar statute to the Acts mentioned in subsection (1) of that section.

(4) Where a hereditament which is not used for the purpose for which it was constructed or has been adapted becomes so used on any day and becomes not so used again on the expiration of a period of less than six weeks beginning with that day, then for the purpose of ascertaining any period during which the hereditament has been continuously not so used, it shall be deemed to have remained not so used on that day and during that period.

(5) A hereditament shall be taken to be used on any day for the purposes for which it was constructed or has been adapted if, but only if, not less than four-fifths of it was so used on that day.

(6) Schedule 1 to this Act (except paragraphs 1, 2 (*c*) and (*d*), 6, 12 and 14) shall apply for the purposes of section 17A of this Act as it applies for the purposes of section 17 thereof, as if—

(*a*) references to paragraph 1 of that Schedule were references to section 17A of this Act,
(*b*) references to a relevant hereditament or a relevant period of vacancy were references to a commercial building and a period of non-use respectively, and
(*c*) references to three months were references to six months.

(7) In section 17A of this Act and this section 'owner' means the person entitled to possession, and where different persons are entitled to possession of a hereditament during different parts of a period of non-use, a surcharge in respect of that period shall be apportioned between them according to the length of each part and levied accordingly.

(8) In the application of section 17A of this Act to the City of London, 'rates' means the aggregate of the poor rate and the general rate.

(9) Section 17A of this Act shall not apply to any period before the passing of the Local Government Act 1974." [**216**]

EXPLANATORY NOTE

This section adds two sections, 17A and 17B to the General Rate Act 1967. The scheme it introduces is compulsory but does not apply to any period before 8th February 1974 (s. 17B (9)). See also paras. [**54**]–[**59**], *ante*.

DEFINITIONS

"Continuous period." See s. 17B (4) for effect of short term letting.
"Commercial building." See s. 17B (2).
"Owner". See s. 17B (7). Cf. General Rate Act 1967, s. 115.
"Rates." See General Rate Act 1967, s. 115 and s. 17B (8).
"Period of non-use." See s. 17A (1).
"Tried his best." See s. 17A (5) for factors to be considered.
"Used." See s. 17B (5).

17. Increases in statutory deduction from gross value: alteration of valuation lists

If, on or before 31st December 1973, a draft of an order is laid before Parliament under subsection (5) of section 19 of the principal Act increasing the amount which, in accordance with subsection (2) of that section, is to be deducted from the gross value of a hereditament of a class specified in the order for the purpose of ascertaining the net annual value of that hereditament and an order is made in terms of the draft so laid—

(*a*) the valuation officer shall, by directions to the rating authority, cause to be made in a valuation list any alterations necessary to give effect to the increased deductions, and the rating authority shall give effect to any such directions accordingly; and

(*b*) any alteration made in a valuation list by virtue of paragraph (*a*) above shall have effect as from 1st April 1974, but without prejudice to any subsequent alteration of the valuation list made by virtue of any provision of the principal Act. [**217**]

EXPLANATORY NOTE

See paras. [**60**], [**61**], *ante*.

ORDER

The Valuation (Statutory Deductions) Order 1973, S.I. 1973 No. 2139, is such an order as is described in this section.

18. Rating of plant and machinery

(1) In subsection (5) of section 21 of the principal Act (power for the Secretary of State by order to exclude certain items of plant or machinery, or parts of such items, from being treated as part of a hereditament for the purposes of valuation) for the words from "which satisfies" to the end of the subsection there shall be substituted the words "which falls within any of paragraphs (*a*) to (*c*) below, that is to say—

(*a*) any item or part of an item which is moved or rotated by motive power as part of a process of manufacture;

(*b*) so much of any refractory or other lining forming part of any plant or machinery as is customarily renewed by reason of normal use at intervals of such frequency being less than a year as may be specified in the order;

(*c*) any item which is of such a description and in respect of which such conditions are fulfilled as may be specified in the order and which is readily capable of being moved from one site and re-erected in its original state on another without the substantial demolition of the item or of any surrounding structure".

(2) Section 22 of the principal Act (determination of certain questions as to plant and machinery) shall cease to have effect. [**218**]

EXPLANATORY NOTE

See para. [**62**], *ante*.

ORDER

As a consequence of the amendments made by this section, the Plant and Machinery (Rating) (Amendment) Order 1974, S.I. 1974 No. 413, has been made under the General Rate Act 1967, s. 21 (5).

19. Rating of certain public utilities and other bodies

(1) The Secretary of State may by order make provision for determining, by such method as may be specified in the order, the rateable value of, or of any class or description of, the hereditaments specified in Schedule 3 to this Act.

(2) An order under this section applying to any hereditament, or any class or description of hereditament, may provide for determining rateable value by the application of different methods of valuation to different parts of the hereditament.

(3) Before making an order under this section the Secretary of State shall consult with such associations of local authorities or of persons carrying on undertakings as appear to him to be concerned and with any local authority or person carrying on an undertaking with whom consultation appears to him to be desirable.

(4) An order under this section may repeal or amend any provision of—

(*a*) sections 31 to 34 of and Schedules 4 to 7 to the principal Act,
(*b*) section 52 of the Post Office Act 1969, and
(*c*) any other provision of the principal Act so far as that provision relates to the valuation of hereditaments to which the order relates,

and any such order may as regards any such hereditaments apply, restrict or modify the provisions of the principal Act relating to proposals for alterations of valuation lists and to appeals in connection with such lists and to the withholding of rates where proposals are pending, and shall have effect notwithstanding anything in any of those provisions.

(5) No order under this section shall have effect unless approved by a resolution of each House of Parliament. [**219**]

EXPLANATORY NOTE

See para. [**63**], *ante*.

DEFINITIONS

"Consult." See note to s. 1, *ante*.
"Principal Act." This is the General Rate Act 1967.
"By order." This is by statutory instrument; see s. 22 (3).

20. Exemption from rates for certain hereditaments comprising facilities for disabled persons

Section 45 of the principal Act (relief in respect of facilities for disabled persons) shall have effect, and shall be deemed to have had effect on and after 1st April 1973, as if at the end of the section there were added the following subsections—

"(2) No person shall, in respect of any period, be liable to pay rates in respect of a hereditament to which this subsection applies, or be deemed to be in occupation thereof for rating purposes, and notwithstanding anything in this Act no such hereditament shall be included in any rate made in respect of any period.

(3) Subsection (2) of this section applies to a hereditament consisting exclusively of—

(*a*) land on which is erected a structure falling within paragraph (*a*) of subsection (1) of this section; or
(*b*) land on which is erected a structure which falls within paragraph (*c*) of subsection (1) of this section and which is provided for the accommodation of a vehicle used by an invalid or disabled person; or
(*c*) land on which is erected a structure which falls within paragraph (*d*) of subsection (1) of this section and is of a kind similar to such a structure as is referred to in paragraph (*a*) or paragraph (*b*) above; or

(*d*) land falling within paragraph (*a*), paragraph (*b*) or paragraph (*c*) above together with other land occupied and used solely in connection with the structure in question; or

(*e*) land on which no structure is erected but which is used exclusively for the keeping of a vehicle used by an invalid or disabled person." [**220**]

EXPLANATORY NOTE

See paras. [**64**] and [**65**], *ante*.

21. Valuation lists not to be altered on account of minor structural alterations to dwellings

(1) In the case of a hereditament which is a dwellinghouse or a mixed hereditament within the meaning of section 48 of the principal Act, no proposal may be made under section 69 of that Act for an increase in the gross value ascribed to the hereditament in the valuation list by reason of the making of structural alterations on or after 1st April 1974—

(*a*) if and so far as the alterations are necessary for the purpose of installing a system for providing heating in two or more rooms in the hereditament, or

(*b*) if the proposal would be for an increase not exceeding such an amount as the Secretary of State may by order specify,

and, accordingly, references in the following provisions of this section to structural alterations do not include alterations falling within paragraph (*a*) above.

(2) If, by reason of the making of structural alterations on or after 1st April 1974, a proposal is made for an increase in the gross value of any such hereditament as is referred to in subsection (1) above, but—

(*a*) an agreement is reached under section 72 (1) of the principal Act on the alteration of the valuation list which, apart from this section, would be appropriate to take account of the alterations, and

(*b*) the alteration so agreed would represent an increase in the gross value of such an amount that, by virtue of subsection (1) (*b*) above, no proposal for an increase of that amount could have been made,

then, notwithstanding the said section 72 (1), no alteration shall be made to the gross value ascribed to the hereditament in the valuation list.

(3) If, by reason of the making of structural alterations on or after 1st April 1974, a proposal is made for an increase in the gross value of any such hereditament as is referred to in subsection (1) above but, on an appeal under section 76 or an arbitration under section 78 of the principal Act relating to the proposal, the court or arbitrator is of the opinion that the increase in the gross value to take account of the alterations would be of such an amount that, by virtue of subsection (1) (*b*) above, no proposal for an increase of that amount could have been made, the court or arbitrator shall direct that no alteration be made to the gross value ascribed to the hereditament in the valuation list.

(4) If, by reason of the making of structural alterations on or after 1st April 1974, the gross value of any such hereditament as is referred to in subsection (1) above is increased but, on an appeal under section 77 of the principal Act, the Lands Tribunal is of the opinion that the increase in the gross value should be reduced to such an amount that, by virtue of subsection (1) (*b*) above, no proposal for an increase of that amount could have been made, the Tribunal shall

give such directions as appear to it to be appropriate to secure that the valuation list is altered so as to restore to the hereditament the gross value ascribed to it in that list before the increase,

(5) In any case where—

(*a*) by virtue of subsection (1) (*b*) above, no proposal for an increase in the gross value ascribed to a hereditament in a valuation list is made to take account of the making of structural alterations, but

(*b*) as a result of subsequent structural alterations, a proposal, permitted by subsection (1) above, is made under section 69 of the principal Act for such an increase,

then, for the purposes of section 79 (2) of the principal Act (date on which alterations in the valuation list are to have effect), the event by reason of which the alteration is made shall be taken to be the making of the last of the structural alterations of which account was taken in the making of the proposal referred to in paragraph (*b*) above.

(6) An order under subsection (1) (*b*) above shall be of no effect unless it is approved by a resolution of each House of Parliament. [**221**]

EXPLANATORY NOTE

See paras. [**66**]–[**69**], *ante*.

DEFINITIONS

"Principal Act." This is the General Rate Act 1967. (Other terms used in this section have the same meaning as in that Act.)

"By order." See note to s. 12, *ante*.

SPECIFIED AMOUNT

The Rating of Minor Structural Alterations to Dwellings (Specified Amount) Order 1974, S.I. 1974 No. 629, specifies an amount of £30 for the purposes of sub-s. (1) (*b*) above.

22. Interpretation of Part II

(1) In this Part of this Act—

"the principal Act" means the General Rate Act 1967;

"local rate rebate scheme" has the meaning assigned to it by section 12 above; and

"the statutory rate rebate scheme" has the meaning assigned to it by section 11 above.

(2) Except in so far as otherwise provided in this Part of this Act, expressions used in this Part have the same meanings as in the principal Act.

(3) Sections 114 (rules, regulations and orders) and 118 (application to Isles of Scilly) of the principal Act shall apply as if this Part of this Act were contained in the principal Act. [**222**]

PART III

LOCAL GOVERNMENT ADMINISTRATION

23. The Commissions for Local Administration

(1) For the purpose of conducting investigations in accordance with this Part of this Act, there shall be—

(*a*) a body of commissioners to be known as the Commission for Local Administration in England, and

(*b*) a body consisting of two or more commissioners to be known as the Commission for Local Administration in Wales.

(2) The Parliamentary Commissioner shall be a member of each of the Commissions.

(3) In the following provisions of this Part of this Act the expression "Local Commissioner" means a person, other than the Parliamentary Commissioner, who is a member of one of the Commissions.

(4) Appointments to the office of Local Commissioner shall be made by Her Majesty on the recommendation of the Secretary of State after consultation with the appropriate representative body, and a person so appointed shall, subject to subsection (6) below, hold office during good behaviour.

(5) Local Commissioners may be appointed to serve either as full-time commissioners or as part-time commissioners.

(6) A Local Commissioner may be relieved of office by Her Majesty at his own request or may be removed from office by Her Majesty on grounds of incapacity or misbehaviour, and shall in any case vacate office on completing the year of service in which he attains the age of sixty-five years.

(7) The Secretary of State shall designate two of the Local Commissioners for England as chairman and vice-chairman respectively of the Commission for Local Administration in England and, in the event of there being more than one Local Commissioner for Wales, shall designate one of them as chairman of the Commission for Local Administration in Wales.

(8) The Commission for Local Administration in England shall divide England into areas and shall provide, in relation to each area, for one or more of the Local Commissioners to be responsible for the area; and where the Commission for Local Administration in Wales consist of more than one Local Commissioner they may, if they think fit, act in a similar way in Wales.

A Local Commissioner may, by virtue of this subsection, be made responsible for more than one area.

(9) It shall be the duty of the Commission for Local Administration in England to ensure that any Local Commissioner made responsible for an area which includes the county of Cornwall is made responsible for an area which also includes the Isles of Scilly.

(10) Each of the Commissions—

(*a*) shall make arrangements for Local Commissioners to accept cases for which they are not responsible including, where the other Commission so request, a case arising in the country of that other Commission, and

(*b*) shall publish information about the procedures for making complaints under this Part of this Act.

(11) For the year ending on 31st March 1975, and for each subsequent financial year, every Local Commissioner shall prepare a general report on the discharge of his functions and shall submit it to his Commission; and where he has discharged functions at the request of the other Commission he shall prepare a general report on the discharge of those functions and shall submit it to the other Commission.

Any such report shall be submitted to the appropriate Commission not later than two months after the end of the year to which it relates.

(12) The Commissions shall each financial year review the operation of the provisions of this Part of this Act about the investigation of complaints, and shall have power to convey to local authorities (through the appropriate representative body designated under section 24 below), or to government departments, any recommendations or conclusions reached in the course of their reviews.

(13) Schedule 4 to this Act shall have effect as respects the Commissions. [**223**]

EXPLANATORY NOTE

See paras. [**70**]–[**78**] for general background; [**79**]–[**87**]; [**142**].

DEFINITIONS

"Wales." See s. 34 (2). The effect is that Wales includes Gwent (formerly Monmouthshire).

"Parliamentary Commissioner." This is the Parliamentary Commissioner for Administration, appointed under the Parliamentary Commissioner Act 1967.

"Representative body". See s. 24 (1) (*c*).

"Local authorities." See s. 34 (1).

"Financial year." This is 1st April to 31st March.

24. Bodies representing authorities to which Part III applies

(1) The Secretary of State shall by order designate bodies to be called respectively "the representative body for England" and "the representative body for Wales".

(2) The said representative bodies shall be bodies appearing to the Secretary of State to represent authorities in England to which this Part of this Act applies, or as the case may be such authorities in Wales.

(3) An order made under subsection (1) above may be varied or revoked by a subsequent order so made, and shall be contained in a statutory instrument subject to annulment in pursuance of a resolution of either House of Parliament.

(4) For the year ending on 31st March 1975, and for each subsequent financial year, each of the Commissions shall prepare a general report on the discharge of their functions and shall submit it to the appropriate representative body.

(5) The report shall be submitted as soon as may be after the Commission have received the reports for the year from Local Commissioners under section 23 (11) above, and each Commission shall submit copies of those reports, together with their own report.

(6) Each representative body shall arrange for the publication of the reports submitted to them under the preceding provisions of this section.

(7) In transmitting to local authorities recommendations or conclusions conveyed by either of the Commissions (in accordance with section 23 (12) above) the representative body concerned may make such comments on those recommendations or conclusions as they think appropriate.

(8) Where, in accordance with subsection (6) above, a representative body arrange for the publication of a report submitted to them under subsection (4) above, they may also arrange for the report to be published with an annex containing such comments on the report as they think appropriate.

(9) Without prejudice to the generality of subsection (8) above, comments made by a representative body by virtue of that subsection may relate to particular classes of authorities to which this Part of this Act applies.

(10) Where the Commission for Local Administration in Wales consist of only one Local Commissioner, section 23 (11) above and subsection (5) above shall have effect with the necessary modifications. [224]

EXPLANATORY NOTE
See paras. [**148**], [**149**], *ante*.

DEFINITION
"Authorities . . . to which this Act applies." See s. 28 (1)–(4).

ORDER
See the Local Government Administration (Representative Body for England) Order 1974, S.I. 1974 No. 683, and, for Wales, No. 707.

25. Authorities subject to investigation

(1) This Part of this Act applies to—

(*a*) any local authority,
(*b*) any joint board the constituent authorities of which are all local authorities,
(*c*) any police authority, other than the Secretary of State, and
(*d*) any water authority within the meaning of the Water Act 1973.

(2) Her Majesty may by Order in Council provide that this Part of this Act shall also apply, subject to any modifications or exceptions specified in the Order, to any authority specified in the Order, being an authority which is established by or under an Act of Parliament, and which has power to levy a rate, or to issue a precept.

(3) An Order made by virtue of subsection (2) above may be varied or revoked by a subsequent Order so made and shall be subject to annulment in pursuance of a resolution of either House of Parliament.

(4) Any reference to an authority to which this Part of this Act applies includes a reference—

(*a*) to the members and officers of that authority, and
(*b*) to any person or body of persons acting for the authority under section 101 or section 110 of the Local Government Act 1972 (arrangements for discharge of functions by local authorities), or
(*c*) any committee mentioned in section 101 (9) of the said Act. [225]

EXPLANATORY NOTE
See paras. [**88**]–[**90**], *ante*.

DEFINITIONS
"Local authority." See s. 34 (1).
"Police authority." See Police Act 1964, as amended by Local Government Act 1972.
"Water authority." See Water Act 1973, s. 2.
"Order in Council." This is by statutory instrument. See Statutory Instruments Act 1946.

26. Matters subject to investigation

(1) Subject to the provisions of this Part of this Act where a written complaint is made by or on behalf of a member of the public who claims to have sustained injustice in consequence of maladministration in connection with action taken by or on behalf of an authority to which this Part of this Act applies, being action taken in the exercise of administrative functions of that authority, a Local Commissioner may investigate that complaint.

(2) A complaint shall not be entertained under this Part of this Act unless—

(*a*) it is made in writing to a member of the authority, or of any other authority concerned, specifying the action alleged to constitute maladministration, and

(*b*) it is referred to the Local Commissioner, with the consent of the person aggrieved, or of a person acting on his behalf, by that member, or by any other person who is a member of any authority concerned, with a request to investigate the complaint.

(3) If the Local Commissioner is satisfied that any member of any authority concerned has been requested to refer the complaint to a Local Commissioner, and has not done so, the Local Commissioner may, if he thinks fit, dispense with the requirements in subsection (2) (*b*) above.

(4) a complaint shall not be entertained unless it was made to a member of any authority concerned within twelve months from the day on which the person aggrieved first had notice of the matters alleged in the complaint, but a Local Commissioner may conduct an investigation pursuant to a complaint not made within that period if he considers that there are special circumstances which make it proper to do so.

(5) Before proceeding to investigate a complaint, a Local Commissioner shall satisfy himself that the complaint has been brought, by or on behalf of the person aggrieved, to the notice of the authority to which the complaint relates and that that authority has been afforded a reasonable opportunity to investigate, and reply to, the complaint.

(6) A Local Commissioner shall not conduct an investigation under this Part of this Act in respect of any of the following matters, that is to say,—

(*a*) any action in respect of which the person aggrieved has or had a right of appeal, reference or review to or before a tribunal constituted by or under any enactment;

(*b*) any action in respect of which the person aggrieved has or had a right of appeal to a Minister of the Crown; or

(*c*) any action in respect of which the person aggrieved has or had a a remedy by way of proceedings in any court of law:

Provided that a Local Commissioner may conduct an investigation notwithstanding the existence of such a right or remedy if satisfied that in the particular circumstances it is not reasonable to expect the person aggrieved to resort or have resorted to it.

(7) A Local Commissioner shall not conduct an investigation in respect of any action which in his opinion affects all or most of the inhabitants of the area of the authority concerned.

(8) Without prejudice to the preceding provisions of this section, a Local Commissioner shall not conduct an investigation under this Part of this Act in respect of any such action or matter as is described in Schedule 5 to this Act.

(9) Her Majesty may by Order in Council amend the said Schedule 5 so as to exclude from the provisions of that Schedule such actions or matters as may be described in the Order; and any Order made by virtue of this subsection shall be subject to annulment in pursuance of a resolution of either House of Parliament.

(10) In determining whether to initiate, continue or discontinue an investigation, a Local Commissioner shall, subject to the preceding provisions of this section, act at discretion; and any question whether a complaint is duly made under this Part of this Act shall be determined by the Local Commissioner.

(11) In this section references to a person aggrieved include references to his personal representatives.

(12) A complaint shall not be entertained under this Part of this Act if and so far as it is in respect of anything done before 1st April 1974, or in respect of any default or alleged default first arising before that date. [**226**]

EXPLANATORY NOTE
See paras. [**91**]–[**107**], *ante*.

DEFINITIONS
"Injustice." This is not defined. See para. [**118**], *ante*.
"Maladministration." This is not defined. See para. [**119**], *ante*.
"Action." This includes failure to act—s. 34 (1).
"An authority to which this Act applies." See s. 25.
"Administrative functions." This is not defined, but the same phrase in the Parliamentary Commissioner Act 1967, s. 5, is taken to exclude judicial and legislative functions. See para. [**92**], *ante*.
"Local Commissioner." See s. 23 (3).
"May." See para. [**125**], *ante*.
"Member of the authority." See s. 34 (1).
"Person aggrieved." This is the person who claims or is alleged (by the person submitting the claim on his behalf) to have sustained the injustice mentioned in this section. It also includes such a person's personal representative (see s. 26 (11)).
"Tribunal." See s. 34 (1), and para. [**94**], *ante*.
"Proceedings in any court of law." See para. [**96**], *ante*.
"Right of appeal." See paras. [**94**], [**95**], *ante*.

COMMENCEMENT
This section came into force on 8th February 1974 but a complaint cannot be considered in respect of anything done or not done before 1st April 1974.

27. Provisions relating to complaints

(1) A complaint under this Part of this Act may be made by any individual, or by any body of persons whether incorporated or not, not being—

(*a*) a local authority or other authority or body constituted for purposes of the public service or of local government, or for the purposes of carrying on under national ownership any industry or undertaking or part of an industry or undertaking;

(*b*) any other authority or body whose members are appointed by Her Majesty or any Minister of the Crown or government department, or whose revenues consist wholly or mainly of moneys provided by Parliament.

(2) Where the person by whom a complaint might have been made under the preceding provisions of this Part of this Act has died or is for any reason unable to act for himself, the complaint may be made by his personal representative or by a member of his family or by some body or individual suitable to represent him; but except as aforesaid a complaint shall not be entertained under this Part of this Act unless made by the person aggrieved himself. [**227**]

EXPLANATORY NOTE
See paras. [**108**]–[**111**], *ante*.

DEFINITIONS
"Local authority." See s. 34 (1).
"Carrying on under national ownership." See para. [**108**], *ante*.
"Person aggrieved himself." See s. 26 (1), *ante*, and para. [**109**], *ante*.

28. Procedure in respect of investigations

(1) Where a Local Commissioner proposes to conduct an investigation pursuant to a complaint, he shall afford to the authority concerned, and to any person who is alleged in the complaint to have taken or authorised the action complained of, an opportunity to comment on any allegations contained in the complaint.

(2) Every such investigation shall be conducted in private, but except as aforesaid the procedure for conducting an investigation shall be such as the Local Commissioner considers appropriate in the circumstances of the case; and without prejudice to the generality of the preceding provision the Local Commissioner may obtain information from such persons and in such manner, and make such inquiries, as he thinks fit, and may determine whether any person may be represented (by counsel or solicitor or otherwise) in the investigation.

(3) The Local Commissioner may, if he thinks fit, pay to the person by whom the complaint was made, and to any other person who attends or furnishes information for the purposes of an investigation under this Part of this Act—

(*a*) sums in respect of the expenses properly incurred by them;

(*b*) allowances by way of compensation for the loss of their time,

in accordance with such scales and subject to such conditions as may be determined by the Minister for the Civil Service.

(4) The conduct of an investigation under this Part of this Act shall not affect any action taken by the authority concerned, or any power or duty of that authority to take further action with respect to any matters subject to the investigation. [**228**]

EXPLANATORY NOTE

See paras. [**123**], [**124**], [**134**]–[**136**], *ante*.

DEFINITION

"Local Commissioner." See s. 23 (3).

29. Investigations: further provisions

(1) For the purposes of an investigation under this Part of this Act a Local Commissioner may require any member or officer of the authority concerned, or any other person who in his opinion is able to furnish information or produce documents relevant to the investigation, to furnish any such information or produce any such documents.

(2) For the purposes of any such investigation a Local Commissioner shall have the same powers as the High Court in respect of the attendance and examination of witnesses, and in respect of the production of documents.

(3) A Local Commissioner may, under subsection (1) above, require any person to furnish information concerning communications between the authority concerned and any Government department, or to produce any correspondence or other documents forming part of any such written communications.

(4) No obligation to maintain secrecy or other restriction upon the disclosure of information obtained by or furnished to persons in Her Majesty's service, whether imposed by any enactment or by any rule of law, shall apply to the disclosure of information in accordance with subsection (3) above; and where that subsection applies the Crown shall not be entitled to any such privilege in

respect of the production of documents or the giving of evidence as is allowed by law in legal proceedings.

(5) Nothing in subsection (1) or subsection (3) above affects—

(*a*) the restriction, imposed by section 11 (2) of the Parliamentary Commissioner Act 1967, on the disclosure of information by the Parliamentary Commissioner or his officers; or

(*b*) the restriction, imposed by that section (as applied by section 36 of the National Health Service Reorganisation Act 1973), on the disclosure of information by the Health Service Commissioner for England or the Health Service Commissioner for Wales, or by their officers.

(6) To assist him in any investigation, a Local Commissioner may obtain advice from any person who in his opinion is qualified to give it and may pay to any such person such fees or allowances as he may determine with the approval of the Minister for the Civil Service.

(7) Subject to subsection (4) above, no person shall be compelled for the purposes of an investigation under this Part of this Act to give any evidence or produce any document which he could not be compelled to give or produce in civil proceedings before the High Court.

(8) If any person without lawful excuse obstructs a Local Commissioner in the performance of his functions under this Part of this Act, or any officer of the Commission assisting in the performance of those functions, or is guilty of any act or omission in relation to an investigation under this Part of this Act which, if that investigation were a proceeding in the High Court, would constitute contempt of court, the Local Commissioner may certify the offence to the High Court.

(9) Where an offence is so certified, the High Court may inquire into the matter and, after hearing any witnesses who may be produced against or on behalf of the person charged with the offence, and after hearing any statement that may be offered in defence, deal with him in any manner in which the High Court could deal with him if he had committed the like offence in relation to the High Court.

(10) Nothing in subsection (8) above shall be construed as applying to the taking of any such action as is mentioned in section 28 (4) above. [**229**]

EXPLANATORY NOTE

See paras. [**126**]–[**133**], *ante*.

SUB-S. (2)

Cf. Parliamentary Commissioner Act 1967, s. 8 (2).

SUB-S. (8)

For acts or omissions which "would constitute contempt of court", see Borrie and Lowe, *The Law of Contempt*

DEFINITION

"Without lawful excuse." For the meaning of this in other contexts see Stroud's Judicial Dictionary, Vol. 3, p. 1496. Its meaning might arise here if a Commissioner required the production of documents and the person in possession thought the matter was one over which the Commissioner had no jurisdiction.

30. Reports on investigations

(1) In any case where a Local Commissioner conducts an investigation, or decides not to conduct an investigation, he shall send a report of the results of the investigation, or as the case may be a statement of his reasons for not conducting an investigation—

(*a*) to the person, if any, who referred the complaint to the Local Commissioner in accordance with section 26 (2) above, and
(*b*) to the complainant, and
(*c*) to the authority concerned, and to any other authority or person who is alleged in the complaint to have taken or authorised the action complained of.

(2) Where the complaint was referred by a person who was a member of an authority but who has since ceased to be a member of that authority, the report or statement shall be sent to the chairman, or, as the case may be, mayor of that authority.

(3) Apart from identifying the authority or authorities concerned, the report shall not—

(*a*) mention the name of any person, or
(*b*) contain any particulars which, in the opinion of the Local Commissioner, are likely to identify any person and can be omitted without impairing the effectiveness of the report,

unless, after taking into account the public interest as well as the interests of the complainant and of persons other than the complainant, the Local Commissioner considers it necessary to mention the name of that person or to include in the report any such particulars.

(4) Subject to the provisions of subsection (7) below, the authority concerned shall for a period of three weeks make copies of the report available for inspection by the public without charge at all reasonable hours at one or more of their offices; and any person shall be entitled to take copies of, or extracts from, the report when so made available.

(5) Not later than one week after the report is received by the authority concerned, the proper officer of the authority shall give public notice, by advertisement in newspapers and such other ways as appear to him appropriate, that the report will be available for inspection as provided by subsection (4) above, and shall specify the date, being a date after the giving of the public notice, from which the period of three weeks will begin.

(6) If a person having the custody of a report made available for inspection as provided by subsection (4) above obstructs any person seeking to inspect the report, or to make a copy of, or extract from, the report, he shall be liable on summary conviction to a fine not exceeding £50.

(7) The Local Commissioner may, if he thinks fit after taking into account the public interest as well as the interests of the complainant and of persons other than the complainant, direct that a report specified in the direction shall not be subject to the provisions of subsections (4) and (5) above about its publication. [**230**]

EXPLANATORY NOTE
See paras. [**137**]–[**139**], *ante*.

DEFINITION
"Proper officer." See Local Government Act 1972, s. 270 (3) and Joint Circular 111/73 (DoE) and 204/73 (Welsh Office).

31. Reports on investigations: further provisions

(1) If in the opinion of the Local Commissioner, as set out in the report, injustice has been caused to the person aggrieved in consequence of maladministration,

the report shall be laid before the authority concerned, and it shall be the duty of that authority to consider the report, and to notify the Local Commissioner of the action which the authority have taken, or propose to take.

(2) If the Local Commissioner—

(*a*) does not receive any such notification within a reasonable time; or

(*b*) is not satisfied with the action which the authority concerned have taken; or

(*c*) does not within a reasonable time receive confirmation from the authority concerned that they have taken action, as proposed, to the satisfaction of the Local Commissioner,

he shall make a further report setting out those facts; and section 30 above shall apply, with any necessary modifications, to that further report. [**231**]

EXPLANATORY NOTE

See paras. [**140**], [**141**], *ante*.

DEFINITIONS

"Injustice." See notes to s. 26, *ante*.
"Maladministration." See notes to s. 26, *ante*.
"Person aggrieved." See notes to s. 26, *ante*.

32. Law of defamation, and disclosure of information

(1) For the purposes of the law of defamation, any such publication as is hereinafter mentioned shall be absolutely privileged, that is to say—

(*a*) the publication of any matter in communications between a member of an authority and a Local Commissioner, or any officer of either Commission, for the purposes of this Part of this Act;

(*b*) the publication of any matter by a Local Commissioner or by any officer of either Commission, in communicating with a complainant for the purposes of this Part of this Act;

(*c*) the publication of any matter in preparing, making and sending a report or statement in accordance with section 30 or section 31 above, or, subject to section 30 (7) above, in making a report available to the public;

(*d*) the publication of any matter contained in a report by a Local Commissioner which has been made available to the public, being publication by inclusion in a report made or published under section 24 above.

(2) Information obtained by a Local Commissioner, or any officer of either Commission, in the course of or for the purposes of an investigation under this Part of this Act shall not be disclosed except—

(*a*) for the purposes of the investigation and of any report to be made under section 30 or section 31 above; or

(*b*) for the purposes of any proceedings for an offence under the Official Secrets Acts 1911 to 1939 alleged to have been committed in respect of information obtained, by virtue of this Part of this Act, by a Local Commissioner or by an officer of either Commission or for an offence of perjury alleged to have been committed in the course of an investigation under this Part of this Act or for the purposes of an inquiry with a view to the taking of such proceedings, or

(*c*) for the purpose of any proceedings under section 29 (9) above,

and a Local Commissioner and the officers of his Commission shall not be called upon to give evidence in any proceedings (other than proceedings within paragraph (*b*) or (*c*) above) of matters coming to his or their knowledge in the course of an investigation under this Part of this Act.

(3) A Minister of the Crown or any of the authorities mentioned in section 25 (1) above may give notice in writing to a Local Commissioner with respect to any document or information specified in the notice, or any class of documents or information so specified, that in the opinion of the Minister, or as the case may be of the authority, the disclosure of that document or information, or of documents or information of that class, would be contrary to the public interest; and where such a notice is given nothing in this Part of this Act shall be construed as authorising or requiring any person to communicate to any other person, or for any purpose, any document or information specified in the notice, or any document or information of a class so specified:

Provided that a notice given under this subsection by any authority may be discharged by the Secretary of State.

(4) Nothing in subsection (3) above shall affect the obligations imposed by subsections (3) and (4) of section 29 above.

(5) Where information is disclosed in accordance with section 29 (3) above, being information which is derived from a communication from a government department, and which has not been made public, a Local Commissioner shall not without the written consent of an officer of the government department make a report which includes all or any of that information unless he has given the department not less than one month's notice in writing of his intention.

(6) The provisions of this section shall apply to the Commissioners of Customs and Excise and Commissioners of Inland Revenue as they apply to a Minister of the Crown. [**232**]

EXPLANATORY NOTE

See paras. [**143**]–[**147**], *ante*.

33. Consultation between Local Commissioner, the Parliamentary Commissioner and the Health Service Commissioners

(1) If, at any stage in the course of conducting an investigation under this Part of this Act, a Local Commissioner forms the opinion that the complaint relates partly to a matter which could be the subject of an investigation—

(*a*) by the Parliamentary Commissioner, in accordance with section 5 of the Act of 1967, or

(*b*) by the Health Service Commissioner for England or the Health Service Commissioner for Wales, in accordance with section 34 of the Act of 1973,

he shall consult with the appropriate Commissioner about the complaint and, if he considers it necessary, inform the person initiating the complaint under this Part of this Act of the steps necessary to initiate a complaint under the Act of 1967 or under Part III of the Act of 1973, as the case may be.

(2) Where, by virtue of subsection (1) above, a Local Commissioner consults the Parliamentary Commissioner or one of the Health Service Commissioners in relation to a complaint under this Part of this Act, he may consult that Commissioner about any matter relating to the complaint, including—

(*a*) the conduct of any investigation into the complaint, and

(*b*) the form, content and publication of any report of the results of such an investigation.

(3) If, at any stage in the course of conducting an investigation under—

(*a*) the Act of 1967, or

(*b*) Part III of the Act of 1973,

the Commissioner conducting the investigation forms the opinion that the complaint relates partly to a matter which could be the subject of an investigation under this Part of this Act, he shall consult with the appropriate Local Commissioner about the complaint and, if he considers it necessary, inform the person initiating the complaint under the Act of 1967 or Part III of the Act of 1973, as the case may be, of the steps necessary to initiate a complaint under this Part of this Act.

(4) Where, by virtue of subsection (3) above, a Local Commissioner is consulted about a complaint under the Act of 1967 or Part III of the Act of 1973, subsection (2) above shall apply (with the necessary modifications) as it applies in relation to consultations held by virtue of subsection (1) above.

(5) Nothing in section 11 (2) of the Act of 1967, in that section as applied by section 36 of the Act of 1973, or in section 32 (2) of this Act (restrictions of disclosure of information) shall apply in relation to the disclosure of information by any of the Commissioners mentioned in this section, or by any of their officers, in the course of consultations held in accordance with this section.

(6) In this section the "Act of 1967" means the Parliamentary Commissioner Act 1967 and the "Act of 1973" means the National Health Service Reorganisation Act 1973. [**233**]

EXPLANATORY NOTE

See paras. [**150**]–[**154**], *ante*.

34. Interpretation of Part III

(1) In this Part of this Act, unless the context otherwise requires—

"action" includes failure to act, and other expressions connoting action shall be construed accordingly.

"the Commissions" means the Commission for Local Administration in England and the Commission for Local Administration in Wales,

"local authority" means a county council, the Greater London Council, a district council, a London borough council, the Common Council of the City of London, or the Council of the Isles of Scilly,

"member", in relation to a joint board, includes a member of any of the constituent authorities of the joint board,

"person aggrieved" means the person who claims or is alleged to have sustained any such injustice as is mentioned in section 26 (1) above,

"Parliamentary Commissioner" means the Parliamentary Commissioner for Administration;

"representative body" means a body designated under section 24 above,

"tribunal" includes the person constituting a tribunal consisting of one person.

(2) Section 269 of the Local Government Act 1972 (which relates to the meaning of "England" and "Wales" in Acts passed after 1st April 1974) shall apply to this Part of this Act as if it had been passed after that date.

(3) It is hereby declared that nothing in this Part of this Act authorises or requires a Local Commissioner to question the merits of a decision taken with-

out maladministration by an authority in the exercise of a discretion vested in that authority. [**234**]

DEFINITION

"Maladministration." See notes to s. 26, *ante*, and para. [**119**], *ante*.

SUB-S. (2)

The effect is that Wales includes Gwent (formerly Monmouthshire).

PART IV

MISCELLANEOUS AND GENERAL

35. Removal or relaxation of controls affecting certain local authority functions

(1) For the purpose of removing or relaxing controls which affect the exercise by local authorities of certain functions, including limits imposed on the amount of the fees which may be charged by local authorities in connection with the issue of licences and the exercise of other functions, the enactments specified in the first column of Schedule 6 to this Act shall have effect subject to the amendments specified in the second column of that Schedule.

(2) Without prejudice to section 43 (4) below, any reference in Schedule 6 to this Act to any enactment includes a reference to that enactment as applied by any other enactment, including a local Act.

(3) Without prejudice to subsection (1) above, the Secretary of State may by order made by statutory instrument make provision for the removal or relaxation of any control, including any such limit as is referred to in subsection (1) above, which affects the exercise of any function by a local authority and which is conferred by or under any enactment on a Minister of the Crown or a body constituted by or under any enactment.

(4) An order made under this section—

(*a*) may be revoked or varied by a further order so made, and

(*b*) may contain such incidental or consequential provisions as appear to the Secretary of State to be appropriate, including provisions amending or repealing or revoking, with or without savings, any enactment passed before this Act and any instrument made under any such enactment.

(5) A statutory instrument containing an order under this section shall be of no effect unless approved by a resolution of each House of Parliament.

(6) In this section "local authority" means any local authority within the meaning of the Local Government Act 1972, the Common Council of the City of London, the Sub-Treasurer of the Inner Temple, the Under Treasurer of the Middle Temple, the Council of the Isles of Scilly, a port health authority, the London Transport Executive and a Passenger Transport Executive. [**235**]

EXPLANATORY NOTE

See para. [**155**], *ante*.

DEFINITION

Local authorities. Note wider definition in sub-s. (6) above.

MAY BY ORDER, ETC.

The power to amend by order an Act, given by sub-s. (4) (*b*) is not uncommon. Such an order is subject to the affirmative procedure (sub-s. 5).

36. Recovery by local authorities of establishment charges

(1) In any case where a local authority—

(*a*) are empowered under any enactment to carry out any works or do any other thing on or in relation to any land or building, and

(*b*) by virtue of that or any other enactment are entitled to recover from any person expenses incurred by them in exercising that power,

the local authority shall be entitled to recover, together with and in like manner as the expenses which are recoverable as mentioned in paragraph (*b*) above, such sum as appears to them to be reasonable in respect of their establishment charges.

(2) The provisions of subsection (1) above shall have effect in substitution for any provision contained in any enactment, including an enactment in a local Act, under which a local authority who have exercised any such power as is referred to in subsection (1) (*a*) above have power to recover any sum in respect of their establishment charges or any element or elements of those charges.

(3) In this section "local authority" has the same meaning as in section 35 above. [**236**]

EXPLANATORY NOTE

See para. [**156**], *ante*.

DEFINITIONS

"Local authorities." Note wider definition, as in s. 35 (6).

"Reasonable." This does not give the authority an unfettered discretion, as shown by, *e.g.*, *Associated Provincial Picture Houses, Ltd.* v. *Wednesbury Corpn.*, [1948] 1 K.B. 223.

37. Extension of power of local authorities to make advances

(1) Section 43 of the Housing (Financial Provisions) Act 1958 (power of local authorities to make advances for certain housing purposes) shall be amended in accordance with the provisions of this section.

(2) At the end of paragraph (*d*) of subsection (1) there shall be added the words "or

(*e*) subject to subsection (2A) below, facilitating the repayment by means of the advance of the amount outstanding on a previous loan made for any of the purposes specified in paragraphs (*a*) to (*d*) above".

(3) After subsection (2) there shall be inserted the following subsection:—

"(2A) An advance shall not be made for the purpose specified in paragraph (*e*) of subsection (1) above unless the local authority or county council satisfy themselves that the primary effect of the advance will be to meet the housing needs of the applicant by enabling him either to retain an interest in the house concerned or to carry out such works in relation to that house as would be eligible for an advance by virtue of paragraph (*c*) or paragraph (*d*) of that subsection."

(4) In paragraph (*c*) of subsection (3) of the section for the words "may provide for repayment being made either by instalments of principal or by an annuity of principal and interest combined" there shall be substituted the words "shall provide for repayment of the principal—

(i) by instalments (of equal or unequal amounts) beginning either on the date of the advance or at a later date, or

(ii) at the end of a fixed period (with or without a provision allowing the local authority or county council to extend that period) or on the happening of a specified event before the end of that period,

and for the payment of instalments of interest throughout the period beginning on the date of the advance and ending when the whole of the principal is repaid".

(5) At the end of the section there shall be added the following subsection—

"(5) If it appears to a local authority or county council that the principal effect of the making of an advance under subsection (1) above in respect of any premises would be to meet the housing needs of the applicant, they may make the advance notwithstanding that it is intended that some part of the premises will be used or, as the case may be, will continue to be used, otherwise than as a dwelling; and accordingly where, by virtue of this subsection, a local authority or county council propose to make an advance in respect of any premises, the premises shall be treated for the purposes of subsections (1) to (4) above as, or as a building to be converted into, a house or houses".

(6) On the coming into operation of this section, no further advances shall be made by local authorities in England and Wales under section 74 of the Housing Act 1969 or section 41 of the Land Compensation Act 1973. [**237**]

EXPLANATORY NOTE

See para. [**157**], *ante*.

38. Collection by local authorities of charges payable in respect of services provided by water authorities

After section 32 of the Water Act 1973 there shall be inserted the following section—

"**32A. Agreement for collection and recovery by local authorities of charges due to water authorities**

(1) A local authority and a water authority may enter into an agreement for the collection and recovery by the local authority on behalf of the water authority of any charges payable for services performed, facilities provided or rights made available in the local authority's area by the water authority.

(2) Without prejudice to any other method of recovery, where an agreement is entered into under subsection (1) above, any charges which, in accordance with the agreement, are to be collected and recovered by the local authority concerned may be demanded, collected and recovered by the local authority in like manner as, and together with, any amount due to the local authority in respect of the general rate.

(3) Where an agreement is entered into under subsection (1) above—

(*a*) rules made by the Secretary of State under subsection (1) (*a*) of section 113 of the General Rate Act 1967 may make such provision with respect to the documents referred to in that subsection, and (*b*) regulations made by the Secretary of State under that Act may make such modifications of the forms in Schedule 12 to that Act,

as he considers appropriate to take account of the provisions of subsection (2) above". [**238**]

EXPLANATORY NOTE
See para. [**158**], *ante*.

39. Compensation for loss of office: extension of cases for which regulations may provide

For subsection (3) of section 259 of the Local Government Act 1972 (regulations providing for compensation for loss of office attributable to that Act may extend to persons whose loss is attributable to any such transfer or relinquishment of functions as is referred to in paragraph (*c*) of the new subsection set out below) there shall be substituted the following subsection:—

"(3) Without prejudice to subsection (1) above, regulations under this section may make provision in relation to persons who suffer loss of employment or loss or diminution of emoluments which is attributable to—

(*a*) the provisions of any such order as is referred to in section 326 (1) of the Public Health Act 1936;

(*b*) an existing local authority ceasing, as respects the whole or any part of their area, to be a food and drugs authority, within the meaning of the Food and Drugs Act 1955;

(*c*) any transfer or relinquishment of functions under any of the provisions of the Public Health Act 1936 which are incorporated in the Food and Drugs Act 1955 or in the Slaughterhouses Act 1974; or

(*d*) the provisions of an order under section 46 of the Children and Young Persons Act 1969;

and, without prejudice to the repeal of any enactment by this Act, regulations making provision for any of the cases specified in paragraphs (*a*) to (*d*) above may provide that the provisions as to compensation made for that case by section 326 of the Public Health Act 1936, section 129 (1) of the Food and Drugs Act 1955 or, as the case may be, paragraph 2 of Schedule 3 to the Children and Young Persons Act 1969 shall not apply in relation to persons to whom the provisions of the regulations apply."
[**239**]

EXPLANATORY NOTE
See para. [**159**], *ante*.

40. Classification of highways

(1) On and after 1st April 1975, a highway or proposed highway which, immediately before that date, is classified under section 27 (2) of the Local Government Act 1966 as a principal road for the purposes of section 235 of the Highways Act 1959, so far as that section relates to the making of advances to local highway authorities, shall cease to be so classified for the purposes of the said section 235 but, except in so far as the Secretary of State otherwise directs, shall continue to be treated as a principal road or a classified road for the purposes of any enactment or instrument (whether passed or made before or after the passing of this Act) which refers to roads or highways classified under any

enactment as principal roads (whether for the purposes of advances under the said section 235 or otherwise) or, as the case may be, to roads or highways classified by the Secretary of State.

(2) The Secretary of State may by order made by statutory instrument assign some other description to the highways which, whether by virtue of subsection (1) above or otherwise, are for the time being treated as principal roads for the purposes of any enactment or instrument.

(3) If an order is made under subsection (2) above then, except in so far as the order otherwise provides, any reference to a principal road in any enactment or instrument passed or made before the order is made shall be construed as a reference to a highway of the description specified in the order.

(4) Nothing in subsection (2) above shall affect the power of the Secretary of State under section 27 (2) of the Local Government Act 1966 to classify particular highways or proposed highways in such manner as he may determine after consultation with the highway authorities concerned.

(5) In this section "highway" and "proposed highway" have the same meanings as in the Highways Act 1959. [**240**]

EXPLANATORY NOTE

See para. [**160**], *ante*.

41. Expenses

There shall be defrayed out of money provided by Parliament—

(*a*) any sums required for the payment of grants under this Act or any other expenses of a Minister under this Act;

(*b*) any increase attributable to the provisions of this Act in the sums payable out of such money under any other Act. [**241**]

42. Minor and consequential amendments and repeals

(1) Schedule 7 to this Act, which contains minor amendments and amendments consequential on the provisions of this Act, shall have effect.

(2) The enactments specified in Schedule 8 to this Act are hereby repealed to the extent specified in the third column of that Schedule. [**242**]

43. Short title, commencement, construction, application and extent

(1) This Act may be cited as the Local Government Act 1974.

(2) Part II, other than sections 16 and 22, and sections 35, 37 and 42 of this Act and Schedules 6 to 8 to this Act shall come into operation on such day as the Secretary of State may by order made by statutory instrument appoint, and different days may be so appointed for different provisions and for different purposes.

(3) An order under subsection (2) above appointing a day for the coming into operation of any provision of Schedules 6 to 8 to this Act may contain such savings with respect to the operation of that provision as appear to the Secretary of State to be appropriate.

(4) Any reference in this Act to any other enactment shall be construed as referring to that enactment as amended by or under any other enactment, including this Act.

(5) In their application to the Isles of Scilly, the provisions of Parts I and IV of this Act shall have effect subject to such modifications as the Secretary of State may by order made by statutory instrument direct.

(6) Except in so far as Schedule 4 to this Act amends the House of Commons Disqualification Act 1957, this Act shall not extend to Scotland or to Northern Ireland. [**243**]

COMMENCEMENT

This Act received the Royal Assent on 8th February 1974.

The Local Government Act 1974 (Commencement No. 1) Order 1974, S.I. 1974 No. 335, made under sub-s. (2) above, provides for the commencement of provisions of this Act, as follows:—

(i) on 4th March 1974, ss. 15, 17, 42 and Sch. 7, paras. 8, 13;

(ii) on 4th April 1974, ss. 11–14, 18–21, 35, 37, Sch. 6 (except paras. 15, 23 (1)), Sch. 7 (except paras. 2, 8, 13) and Sch. 8 (except the entries relating to ss. 97 and 98 of the National Parks and Access to the Countryside Act 1949, the Weights and Measures Act 1963, the Rating Act 1966, ss. 1 to 5, 8, 10 and 27 (2) of and Schedule 1 to the Local Government Act 1966, s. 49 of and Sch. 9 to the General Rate Act 1967, ss. 72 (6) (*a*) and 84B (8) (*a*) of the Road Traffic Regulation Act 1967, ss. 33 to 35 and 36 of the Countryside Act 1968, ss. 13 (7), 34 (2) and (3) and 138 (6) of the Transport Act 1968, ss. 3 (1), 7 (5) (6) and 29 (1) (*a*) of the Transport (London) Act 1969, the Highways Act 1971, s. 212 (1) of the Town and Country Planning Act 1971, the Housing Finance Act 1972, s. 203 (5) of and para. 12 of Sch. 24 to the Local Government Act 1972, and the Rate Rebate Act 1973;

(iii) on 1st October 1974, Sch. 6, para. 15 and in Sch. 8, the entries relating to the Weights and Measures Act 1963;

(iv) on 1st April 1975, Sch. 6, para. 23 (1), Sch. 7, para. 2 and in Sch. 8, the entries relating to s. 27 (2) of the Local Government Act 1966, ss. 72 (6) (*a*) and 84B (8) (*a*) of the Road Traffic Regulation Act 1967, ss. 34 (2) and (3) of the Transport Act 1968, ss. 7 (5) and (6) and 29 (1) (*a*) of the Transport (London) Act 1969, the Highways Act 1971 and s. 212 (1) of the Town and Country Planning Act 1971.

SCHEDULES

Sections 1, 6 and 8

SCHEDULE 1

TERMINATION OR MODIFICATION OF CERTAIN EXISTING GRANTS

PART I

EXISTING RATE SUPPORT GRANTS

1. The provisions of sections 1 to 5 of the Local Government Act 1966 (in this Part of this Schedule referred to as "the 1966 Act") shall not have effect with respect to any year beginning on or after 1st April 1974 but, subject to paragraph 2 below, nothing in this Act shall affect the continued operation of those provisions on or after that date in relation to any year ending before that date.

2. No order shall be made after 31st March 1974 under section 3 of the 1966 Act (power of Secretary of State to vary rate support grant orders).

3. Without prejudice to his powers under section 4 of this Act, if at any time during the year 1974–75 it appears to the Secretary of State that, but for the provisions of paragraph 2 above, he would have made an order under section 3 of the 1966 Act increasing the amount fixed by the rate support grant order for the year 1973–74 as the aggregate amount of the rate support grants for that year, he may by an order made in like manner and subject to the like provisions as a rate support grant order—

(*a*) increase the amount fixed by the rate support grant order for the year 1974–75 as the estimated aggregate amount of the rate support grants for that year by an amount equal to the increase for which he would have made provision in the order under section 3 of the 1966 Act; and

(*b*) make such increases in all or any of the elements of rate support grants for that year as appear to him to be appropriate in consequence of the increase in the estimated aggregate amount of those grants made by virtue of sub-paragraph (*a*) above.

4. Without prejudice to the generality of the power to make regulations under section 5 of the 1966 Act (for carrying into effect the provisions of sections 1 to 4 of, and Schedule 1 to, that Act) regulations under that section may make—

(*a*) such provision as the Secretary of State considers appropriate, having regard to paragraphs 1 and 2 above, to secure that any calculations or estimates for the time being treated by virtue of any such regulations as provisional are treated on and after 1st April 1974 as conclusive; and

(*b*) such other incidental or consequential provisions, including provisions amending Part I of Schedule 1 to the 1966 Act, as the Secretary of State considers appropriate for, or in connection with, carrying the provisions of this Part of this Schedule into effect.

5. In this Part of this Schedule the expressions "rate support grants" and "rate support grant order" have, in relation to any year ending before 1st April 1974, the same meanings as in the 1966 Act. [**244**]

NOTE

For ministerial explanation of reference to the 1966 Act in para. 4 (*b*) above, see H. of C. Official Report S.C.A., 4th December 1973, col. 222.

Part II

Existing Grants for Highways and Public Transport

6. Subject to paragraph 8 below, on and after 1st April 1975 the power of the Secretary of State—

(*a*) to make advances to a local highway authority under section 235 (1) of the Highways Act 1959 (for the purposes of, or in connection with, highways, road-ferries and the provision of facilities associated with highways), and

(*b*) to make grants to a Passenger Transport Executive under section 20 (8) of the Transport Act 1968 (towards expenditure incurred by the Executive for certain areas in pursuance of agreements with the Railways Board for the provision of railway passenger services), and

(*c*) to make grants to any person under section 56 (1) of the Transport Act 1968 (towards capital expenditure incurred or to be incurred in the provision, improvement or development of facilities for public passenger transport),

shall cease to be exercisable except in cases where it appears to the Secretary of State that, notwithstanding the grants for which provision is made in Part I of this Act, the whole or any part of any expenditure in respect of which any such advances or grants as are referred to in paragraph (*a*), paragraph (*b*) or paragraph (*c*) above could be made should not fall on the local highway authority, Passenger Transport Executive or other person concerned.

7. No grants shall be paid under section 34 (2) of the Transport Act 1968 (towards expenditure incurred by local authorities in making grants to provide assistance for rural bus or ferry services and in the provision of such ferry services) in respect of expenditure incurred in connection with the provision, improvement or continuance, after the end of the year, 1974–75, of any bus service or ferry service, within the meaning of that Act.

8.—(1) In any case where it appears to the Secretary of State—

(*a*) that any person other than a local authority, a Passenger Transport Executive or the London Transport Executive has before 1st April 1975 entered upon a course of expenditure of a capital nature such as is referred to in section 56 (1) of the Transport Act 1968, and

(*b*) that the course of expenditure was entered upon in reliance on an undertaking by the Secretary of State to make a grant or grants towards that expenditure under that section,

then, notwithstanding anything in paragraph 6 above, the Secretary of State may, on or after 1st April 1975, make to that person under that section any grant which he considers appropriate in the light of that undertaking.

(2) In sub-paragraph (1) (*a*) above "local authority" includes the council of an administrative county, county borough or county district.

9.—(1) In any case where it appears to the Secretary of State—

(*a*) that a Passenger Transport Executive or the London Transport Executive has before 1st April 1975 entered upon a course of expenditure of a capital nature such as is referred to in section 56 (1) of the Transport Act 1968, and

(*b*) that the course of expenditure was entered upon in reliance on an undertaking by the Secretary of State to make a grant or grants towards that expenditure under that section,

the Secretary of State shall, as soon as practicable after 1st April 1975, give notice in writing to the appropriate local authority specifying the purpose of the expenditure, the Executive carrying it out and particulars of the grant or grants to which the undertaking relates, including the terms and conditions upon which the grant or grants were to be made and details of the amount or proportion thereof already paid at that date.

(2) An authority to whom a notice is given under sub-paragraph (1) above shall make to the Executive specified in the notice payments under subsection (2) of section 56 of the Transport Act 1968—

(*a*) corresponding in amount to the payments which, in accordance with the particulars specified in the notice, would have been made under the grant or grants concerned, and

(*b*) on terms and conditions corresponding, as near as may be, to those so specified,

and, in relation to the authority, expenditure for the purpose specified in the notice shall be conclusively presumed for the purposes of that subsection to be expenditure towards which payments may be made under that subsection.

(3) In sub-paragraph (1) above "the appropriate local authority", in relation to a Passenger Transport Executive, means the county council which is the Passenger Transport Authority for the Executive's area and, in relation to the London Transport Executive, means the Greater London Council. [**245**]

NOTE

For ministerial explanation of certain transitional arrangements in relation to transport grants see H. of C. Official Report S.C.A., 4th December 1973, cols. 223–4.

PART III

EXISTING GRANTS FOR OTHER SPECIFIC PURPOSES

10. No grants shall be paid for the year 1974–75 or any subsequent year under—

(*a*) section 97 of the National Parks and Access to the Countryside Act 1949 (grants to local authorities in respect of expenditure on National Parks and areas of outstanding natural beauty) except in so far as that section provides for grants in respect of expenditure incurred in the exercise of powers under section 89 (2) of that Act (derelict land) or of powers of acquiring land, whether by agreement or compulsorily, for the purpose of functions under that section;

(*b*) section 98 of that Act (grants to local authorities in respect of expenditure on long-distance routes);

(*c*) section 9 of the Rating Act 1966 (grants to rating authorities in respect of rebates afforded by them under existing rate rebate schemes);

(*d*) section 8 or section 10 of the Local Government Act 1966 (grants to local authorities in respect of expenditure on public open spaces and port health and airport health functions); or

(*e*) section 33, section 34 or section 35 of the Countryside Act 1968 (grants to local authorities and other bodies in respect of expenditure on country parks, including the Lee Valley Regional Park, and the countryside).

11.—(1) The Secretary of State may from time to time, by order made by statutory instrument, provide that, with effect from such year as may be specified in the order, no grant shall be paid under any such local authority grant provision as may be so specified or that no grant shall be so paid except in respect of expenditure of a description so specified.

(2) In this paragraph "local authority grant provision" means an enactment providing for the payment of grants to local authorities (within the meaning of the enactment concerned) in respect of expenditure incurred in connection with a specific function.

(3) An order under this paragraph may contain such provisions as appear to the Secretary of State to be necessary or proper in consequence of the termination of the grants, including provision amending, repealing or revoking, with or without savings, any enactment or instrument made under an enactment.

(4) No order under this paragraph shall have effect unless it is approved by a resolution of each House of Parliament. [**246**]

SCHEDULE 2

ELEMENTS OF RATE SUPPORT GRANTS

PART I

THE NEEDS ELEMENT

1. Subject to paragraph 3 below, the amount of the needs element payable for any year to a local authority shall be the aggregate of—

(*a*) an amount arrived at by multiplying a prescribed sum by the population of the authority's area; and

(*b*) additional amounts determined in such manner as may be prescribed and attributable to such additional factors as may be prescribed for that year.

2. For the purposes of paragraph 1 above the Secretary of State may by regulations provide for the method of determining, for any year—

(*a*) the population of a local authority's area; and

(*b*) the application or operation of any additional prescribed factor in relation to a local authority.

3.—(1) The needs element shall be subject to adjustment, in accordance with the following provisions of this paragraph, in respect of expenditure to which this paragraph applies.

(2) The Secretary of State may by regulations provide for ascertaining the aggregate of the expenditure to which this paragraph applies of all local authorities, for apportioning the aggregate among the authorities and for ascertaining the amount by which the needs element payable to each authority ought to be increased or decreased.

(3) The Secretary of State shall, in accordance with regulations made by him under this paragraph, ascertain at such time as may be specified by the regulations—

(*a*) the estimated amount of the increases and decreases of the needs element which ought to be made for any year, and

(*b*) the actual amount of those increases and decreases,

and he shall in paying the needs element for any year adjust the amount of that element in accordance with the estimated amounts so ascertained and shall in paying that element for the earliest practicable subsequent year make any adjustment necessary to offset differences between the estimated and actual amounts so ascertained.

(4) Subject to sub-paragraph (5) below, this paragraph applies to expenditure incurred—

(*a*) in establishing, maintaining or assisting colleges or other institutions for the training of teachers or in providing or assisting the provision of other facilities specified in directions under section 62 of the Education Act 1944;

(*b*) in making payments, in such cases as may be specified by regulations made by the Secretary of State under this paragraph, to or in respect of persons taking teachers' training or further training courses;

(*c*) in the provision, or in assisting the provision, of such facilities for further education of an advanced character as may be specified by or under regulations so made;

(*d*) in the making of provision for primary, secondary or further education of pupils not belonging to the area of any local education authority;

(*e*) in the training of persons to undertake educational research or to become educational psychologists, or in respect of persons who are being so trained.

(5) The Secretary of State may by regulations provide—

(*a*) that this paragraph shall apply to such expenditure as may be specified by the regulations which is incurred by local authorities—

(i) upon research into any of their functions, or

(ii) in the training of persons in matters connected with the functions of local authorities, or

(iii) in respect of persons to whom the training is given, or

(iv) in providing, for persons who suffer from any disability of mind or body, education by special methods appropriate for persons suffering from that disability, or

(v) in making payments to persons who cease to be employed as teachers in colleges for the training of teachers and become employed either by a local authority in a different capacity or as teachers in voluntary schools; or

(*b*) that any expenditure to which this paragraph applies shall cease to be such expenditure.

4. If, when the needs element for any year falls to be paid, it appears to the Secretary of State that the aggregate amount of that element will exceed or fall short of its aggregate amount as fixed by the relevant rate support grant order, the Secretary of State shall adjust the amount of that element payable to each local authority as nearly as may be in the proportion which the aggregate amount of the element as so fixed bears to the amount, as estimated by the Secretary of State, which would be the aggregate amount of that element for that year apart from this paragraph. [**247**]

EXPLANATORY NOTE

See paras. [**8**]–[**12**], *ante*.

METHODS OF DETERMINING AREA AND POPULATION

See the Rate Support Grant Regulations 1974, S.I. 1974 s. 428, reg. 6.

PART II

THE DOMESTIC ELEMENT

5.—(1) In each year an amount in the pound shall be prescribed for the purposes of section 48 of the General Rate Act 1967 (reduction of rates on dwellings by reference to domestic element) and different amounts in the pound may be so prescribed for different rating areas.

(2) In prescribing any amount or amounts in the pound under this paragraph for any year the Secretary of State shall seek to secure that the total amount of the reductions under section 48 of the General Rate Act 1967 for all rating areas will correspond to the aggregate amount of the domestic element prescribed for that year in pursuance of section 2 (1) of this Act.

(3) In this paragraph "rating area" has the same meaning as in the General Rate Act 1967.

6. The amount of the domestic element payable to a local authority for any year shall be determined in such manner as may be provided by regulations made by the Secretary of State. **[248]**

EXPLANATORY NOTE

See para. [**13**], *ante*.

DETERMINATION OF AMOUNT OF DOMESTIC ELEMENT

See the Rate Support Grant Regulations 1974, S.I. 1974 No. 428, reg. 10.

PART III

THE RESOURCES ELEMENT

7. No payment in respect of the resources element shall be made to a local authority for any year unless in that year the rateable value per head of population of the authority's area is less than the national standard rateable value per head of population.

8. In relation to the resources element, the national standard rateable value per head of population shall be of such amount as may be prescribed.

9.—(1) In relation to the resources element, the rateable value per head of population of the area of a local authority for any year shall be determined by—

(*a*) ascertaining the aggregate of the effective rateable values of all the hereditaments in the area of the authority, including any hereditament which, by virtue of any enactment, any body is to be treated as occupying in that area; and

(*b*) dividing the aggregate figure so ascertained by the population of the authority's area, determined for that year in accordance with regulations made by the Secretary of State.

(2) For the purposes of sub-paragraph (1) above, "effective rateable value", in relation to any hereditament, means such value as may be determined in accordance with regulations made by the Secretary of State; and any such regulations may make different provision in relation to different types of hereditament.

10.—(1) Subject to any provision made by virtue of section 4 (5) of this Act and to paragraph 11 below, the amount of the resources element payable to a local authority for any year shall be an amount arrived at by multiplying the local deficiency in rateable value for that year by the amount in the pound which in accordance with sub-paragraph (3) below is determined as the uniform rate in that year for the authority's area.

(2) For the purposes of sub-paragraph (1) above, "local deficiency in rateable value", in relation to any authority for any year, means the product of—

(*a*) the amount by which, in that year, the national standard rateable value per head of population exceeds the rateable value per head of population of the authority's area; and

(*b*) the population of the authority's area, determined for that year as mentioned in paragraph 9 (1) (*b*) above.

(3) For the purposes of sub-paragraph (1) above "the uniform rate" in any year for the area of a local authority means the amount in the pound determined by dividing—

(*a*) so much of the total estimated expenditure to be incurred by the authority during that year (as mentioned in section 2 (1) of the General Rate Act 1967) as falls to be met by the authority out of the general rate for that year, by

(*b*) the aggregate of the effective rateable values of all the hereditaments in the area of the authority determined as for the purposes of paragraph 9 (1) above.

11.—(1) If, after the amount of the resources element payable to a local authority for any year has been determined under paragraph 10 above,—

(*a*) the rateable values of hereditaments in the authority's area are reduced with effect from a date on or before that which is relevant for determining the aggregate of the effective rateable values of all the hereditaments in the authority's area for that year under paragraph 9 above, and

(*b*) the effect of that reduction is to produce a reduction in the aggregate of the effective rateable values of all the hereditaments in the authority's area which is of such a magnitude that, expressed as a percentage of the initially ascertained aggregate figure, it exceeds such percentage as may be specified for the purposes of this paragraph in regulations made by the Secretary of State, and

(*c*) the authority by notice in writing request the Secretary of State to give a direction under this paragraph,

the Secretary of State shall direct that the amount of the resources element payable to the authority for that year shall be recalculated in accordance with the following provisions of this paragraph and a further payment on account of that element shall be made to the local authority accordingly.

(2) Where sub-paragraph (1) above applies—

(*a*) the rateable value per head of population of the local authority's area for the year concerned shall be recalculated under paragraph 9 above by treating the initially ascertained aggregate figure as reduced by the amount of the excess referred to in sub-paragraph (1) (*b*) above; and

(*b*) subject to any provision made by virtue of section 4 (5) of this Act, paragraph 10 above shall have effect accordingly for the purpose of determining the amount which, on the basis of that recalculation, would have been payable to the authority for that year.

(3) The further payment referred to in sub-paragraph (1) above shall be an amount equal to the difference between the amount previously paid to the authority for the year concerned on account of the resources element and the amount determined as mentioned in sub-paragraph (2) (*b*) above.

(4) In this paragraph "the initially ascertained aggregate figure", in relation to any year, means the aggregate figure ascertained under paragraph 9 (1) (*a*) above for the purposes of the first determination of the amount of the resources element payable to the authority in that year.

(5) The provisions of this paragraph shall have effect notwithstanding that the actual aggregate amount of the resources element for the year concerned may have been specified in an order under section 4 (1) of this Act, and if any amount has been so specified it shall be treated as having been increased to such amount as may be

necessary to provide for any further payment made to a local authority under this paragraph. [**249**]

EXPLANATORY NOTE

See paras. [**14**] to [**18**], *ante*.

EFFECTIVE RATEABLE VALUE

See the Rate Support Grant Regulations 1974, S.I. 1974 No. 428, reg. 9 (1)–(4).

PERCENTAGE SPECIFIED

The percentage specified under para. 11 (1) (*b*) above is 3 per cent.; see reg. 9 (5) of the regulations cited in the preceding note.

SCHEDULE 3

Section 19

Hereditaments to which Section 19 (1) Applies

1. Any water hereditament, within the meaning of section 31 of the principal Act.

2. Any hereditament consisting of railway or canal premises, within the meaning of section 32 of the principal Act, which are occupied wholly or partly for non-rateable purposes of any transport Board, within the meaning of that section.

3. Any hereditament which the British Gas Corporation are to be treated as occupying in a rating area by virtue of section 33 (3) of the principal Act.

4. Any hereditament which an Electricity Board, within the meaning of section 34 of the principal Act, are to be treated as occupying in a rating area by virtue of subsection (3) of that section.

5. Any hereditament occupied by the Post Office by any such property as follows, namely—

(*a*) posts, wires, underground cables and ducts, telephone kiosks and other equipment not within a building, being property used for the purposes of telecommunication services; and

(*b*) the railway constructed, and the works executed, by the Postmaster General in exercise of the powers conferred by the Post Office (London) Railway Act 1913, and the railway constructed, and the works associated therewith executed, by him in exercise of the powers conferred by the Post Office (Site and Railway) Act 1954.

6. Any hereditament occupied by the National Coal Board.

7.—(1) Any other hereditament which consists of or includes a mine or quarry or the whole or part of which is occupied together with a mine or quarry in connection with its working, or the treatment, preparation, storage or removal of its minerals or products of its minerals or the removal of its refuse.

(2) Any reference in sub-paragraph (1) above to a mine or quarry includes a reference to a well or bore-hole or a well and bore-hole combined.

(3) Subject to sub-paragraph (2) above, expressions used in sub-paragraph (1) above and in the Mines and Quarries Act 1954 have the same meanings in sub-paragraph (1) above as in that Act.

8. Any hereditament occupied by the persons carrying on, under authority conferred by or under any enactment, a dock or harbour undertaking.

9. Any hereditament occupied by the persons carrying on an undertaking for the diffusion by wire of sound or television programmes. [**250**]

EXPLANATORY NOTE

See paras. [**63**], *ante*.

SCHEDULE 4

Section 23

THE COMMISSIONS

Disqualifications

1.—(1) A person shall be disqualified for being appointed as, or for being, a Local Commissioner if—

(*a*) he is disqualified for being elected, or being, a member of any of the authorities mentioned in section 25 (1) of this Act; or

(*b*) he is a member of any of those authorities or is a member (by co-option) of a committee of any of those authorities.

(2) A Local Commissioner shall not at any time conduct a case arising in an area if it is wholly or partly within an area for which one of those authorities is responsible and, within the five years ending at that time, the Local Commissioner has been a member of that authority, or a member (by co-option) of a committee of that authority.

(3) The acts and proceedings of a person appointed as a Local Commissioner and acting in that office shall, notwithstanding his disqualification under this paragraph, be as valid and effectual as if he had been qualified.

2.—(1) So long as a Local Commissioner is responsible for any area, and for three years after he ceases to be so responsible, he shall be disqualified for being appointed to any paid office by any of the authorities mentioned in section 25 (1) of this Act if the area for which the Local Commissioner is, or was, responsible falls wholly or partly within the area for which that authority is responsible.

(2) In this paragraph references to the area for which a Local Commissioner is responsible are references to an area for which he assumes responsibility under section 23 of this Act and, if the Commission for Local Administration in Wales consist of more than one Local Commissioner but Wales has not been divided into areas under that section, each of the Local Commissioners for Wales shall be treated as responsible for the whole of Wales. [**251**]

Remuneration, etc.

3.—(1) Each Commission shall pay to or in respect of their Local Commissioners and their officers such amounts, by way of remuneration, pensions, allowances or gratuities or by way of provision for any such benefits, as the Secretary of State may, with the approval of the Minister for the Civil Service, determine.

(2) If a person ceases to be a Local Commissioner and it appears to the Secretary of State that there are special circumstances which make it right that that person should receive compensation, the appropriate Commission may pay to that person a sum of such amount as the Secretary of State may, with the consent of the Minister for the Civil Service, determine. [**252**]

Staff and accommodation

4.—(1) Each of the Commissions may appoint a secretary, and such other officers as they may consider to be required for the discharge of their functions.

(2) Each of the Commissions shall make arrangements to enable Local Commissioners to investigate complaints, and in particular arrangements for—

(*a*) allocating members of their staff to assist Local Commissioners, and

(*b*) providing offices and other accommodation.

(3) An officer of a Commission shall not be allocated to assist a Local Commissioner without the approval of that Local Commissioner.

(4) The Commission for Wales shall ensure that staff are available who can enable a Local Commissioner to deal with complaints in the Welsh language.

(5) Any function of a Local Commissioner, other than that of making any report, may be performed by any officer of the Commission who is authorised for the purpose by the Local Commissioner. [**253**]

Proceedings of the Commissions

5.—(1) The Commissions may determine their own procedure, including the quorum necessary for their meetings.

(2) The validity of any proceedings of either Commission shall not be affected by any vacancy among the members of the Commission or by any defect in the appointment of any member of the Commission.

(3) Each of the Commissions shall be a body corporate, and their common seal shall be authenticated by the signature of a member of the Commission, or of some other person authorised in that behalf by the Commission. [**254**]

Expenses of the Commissions

6. Subject to paragraph 9 below, all expenses incurred by the Commission for Local Administration in England shall be defrayed by the county councils in England, the Greater London Council and the Council of the Isles of Scilly.

7. Subject to paragraph 9 below, all expenses incurred by the Commission for Local Administration in Wales shall be defrayed by the county councils in Wales.

8.—(1) The said expenses shall be apportioned among the authorities liable to defray them, each authority being liable for the fraction $\frac{A}{B}$ of the expenses where—

A is the product of a rate levied in the authority's area of 1p in the pound, as ascertained for the purposes of this paragraph by rules made under section 113 of the General Rate Act 1967, and

B is the aggregate product of a rate levied in the area of every authority in England or, as the case may be, in Wales, of 1p in the pound as so ascertained.

(2) Any sums due to a Commission under this Schedule shall be payable on demand and recoverable as a civil debt; and a Commission may, for any financial year, demand payment in advance of part of their expenses.

9.—(1) In relation to each of the Commissions, the Secretary of State may by order provide for such part of their expenses as may be specified in the order to be defrayed by such authorities (being authorities to which this Part of this Act applies other than those mentioned in paragraph 6 or 7 above) as may be so specified.

(2) Where two or more authorities are liable, by virtue of an order made under this paragraph, to defray part of the expenses of a Commission, the order shall provide for the apportionment of the amount concerned among those authorities.

(3) Paragraphs 6 and 7 above shall not apply in relation to so much of the expenses of a Commission as is, by virtue of any order made under this paragraph, to be defrayed by authorities other than those mentioned in those paragraphs.

(4) An order made under this paragraph shall be contained in a statutory instrument and may be varied or revoked by a subsequent order.

10.—(1) In each financial year each Commission shall prepare an estimate of the expenses which they will incur in the next financial year, and shall submit it, not later than 1st November in the first of those financial years, for consideration by the appropriate representative body.

(2) Any observations by the representative body shall be submitted to the Commission within one month of receipt of the estimate, and it shall be the duty of the Commission to take any such observations into consideration before taking any final decision affecting their expenditure for the next financial year.

(3) The Commission shall, within fourteen days of taking any final decision as to

the estimate for the next financial year, notify the appropriate representative body of the decision.

11.—(1) Where—

(*a*) a representative body have made observations on the estimate submitted to them in accordance with paragraph 10 (1) above;

(*b*) the Commission concerned have notified the representative body of their final decision, in accordance with paragraph 10 (3) above; and

(*c*) the representative body consider that the estimate is excessive;

the representative body may refer the question to the Secretary of State.

(2) Where any question has been referred to the Secretary of State under sub-paragraph (1) above he may, if he considers that the expenditure of the Commission for the next financial year is, on the basis of the estimate, likely to be excessive, give such a direction to the Commission in relation to any matter affecting that expenditure as he considers necessary to ensure that it is not excessive.

(3) It shall be the duty of each of the Commissions to comply with any direction given to them by the Secretary of State under this paragraph.

(4) Any direction given by the Secretary of State under this paragraph may be varied or revoked by a subsequent direction given by him. [**255**]

House of Commons Disqualification Act 1957

12. In Part II of Schedule 1 to the House of Commons Disqualification Act 1957 (bodies of which all members are disqualified under that Act) there shall (at the appropriate place in alphabetical order) be inserted the following entries:—

"The Commission for Local Administration in England".
"The Commission for Local Administration in Wales".

and the like amendments shall be made in the Part substituted for the said Part II by Schedule 3 to that Act in its application to the Northern Ireland Assembly. [**256**]

EXPLANATORY NOTE

See paras. [**79**]–[**87**], *ante*.

SCHEDULE 5

Section 26

MATTERS NOT SUBJECT TO INVESTIGATION

1. The commencement or conduct of civil or criminal proceedings before any court of law.

2. Action taken by any authority in connection with the investigation or prevention of crime.

3.—(1) Action taken in matters relating to contractual or other commercial transactions of any authority to which Part III of this Act applies, including transactions falling within sub-paragraph (2) below but excluding transactions falling within sub-paragraph (3) below.

(2) The transactions mentioned in sub-paragraph (1) above as included in the matters which, by virtue of that sub-paragraph, are not subject to investigation are all transactions of an authority to which Part III of this Act applies relating to the operation of public passenger transport, the carrying on of a dock or harbour undertaking, the provision of entertainment, or the provision and operation of industrial establishments and of markets.

(3) The transactions mentioned in sub-paragraph (1) above as not included in those matters are—

(*a*) transactions for or relating to the acquisition or disposal of land; and (*b*) all transactions (not being transactions falling within sub-paragraph (2) above) in the discharge of functions exercisable under any public general Act, other than those required for the procurement of the goods and services necessary to discharge those functions.

4. Action taken in respect of appointments or removals, pay, discipline, superannuation or other personnel matters.

5.—(1) Any action taken by a local education authority in the exercise of functions under section 23 of the Education Act 1944 (secular instruction in county schools and in voluntary schools).

(2) Any action concerning—

(*a*) the giving of instruction, whether secular or religious, or

(*b*) conduct, curriculum, internal organisation, management or discipline, whether—

(i) in any school maintained by the authority, or

(ii) in any college of education or establishment of further education maintained by the authority. **[257]**

EXPLANATORY NOTE

See paras. [**99**]–[**105**], *ante*.

SCHEDULE 6

Section 35

RELAXATION AND REMOVAL OF CONTROLS

Enactment relating to local authority function	*Amendment*
1. Section 94 of the Public Health Acts Amendment Act 1907 (power of local authorities to license pleasure boats and boatmen).	In subsection (1), for the words from "annual fees" to the end of the subsection there shall be substituted the words "for each type of licence such annual fee as appears to them to be appropriate".
2.—(1) Section 1 of the Performing Animals (Regulation) Act 1925 (restriction on exhibition and training of performing animals).	In subsection (2), for the words "the prescribed fee" there shall be substituted the words "such fee as appears to the local authority to be appropriate"; in subsection (5) the words "on payment of the prescribed fee", in both places where they occur, shall be omitted; in subsection (7) the words "subject to payment of the prescribed fee" shall be omitted; and at the end of the section there shall be added the following subsection: "(8) A local authority may charge such fees as appear to them to be appropriate for inspection of the register, for taking copies thereof or making extracts therefrom or for inspection of copies of certificates of registration issued by them".
(2) Section 5 (3) of that Act (expenses of local authorities, etc.).	The words from "and the fee for registration" to the end shall be omitted.

Enactment relating to local authority function	*Amendment*
3. Section 3 of the Home Counties (Music and Dancing) Licensing Act 1926 (grants and conditions of licences).	For subsection (5) there shall be substituted the following subsection:— "(5) On applications for the grant or transfer of licences there shall be payable such fees as the council may determine, and the council may determine a lower rate of fee for an application for a licence to be granted for the sole purpose of a charitable entertainment."
4. Section 3 of the Civic Restaurants Act 1947 (financial provisions).	In subsection (1) (every civic restaurant authority to keep an account of income and expenditure on income account, and form of that account and particulars to be included therein to be prescribed by Minister of Agriculture, Fisheries and Food) the words from "and the form of the account" to the end of the subsection shall be omitted and in subsection (2) (every civic restaurant authority to endeavour to ensure that their income under the Act is sufficient to defray their expenditure thereunder and if their account shows a deficit for three consecutive financial years their powers to cease to be exercisable) the words from "and if the account" to the end of the subsection shall be omitted.
5. Section 138 of the Local Government Act 1948 (power for local authorities to enter into agreements to assist in performing functions transferred to certain statutory bodies).	Subsection (2) (certain agreements to require prior Ministerial approval) shall be omitted.
6.—(1) Section 64 of the National Parks and Access to the Countryside Act 1949 (power of local planning authority to make access agreements with landowners in their area).	In subsection (1) the words "with the approval of the Minister" shall be omitted.
(2) Section 65 of that Act (power of local planning authorities to make access orders).	Subsection (6) (power of Secretary of State to direct a local planning authority to make an access order or to make such an order himself) shall be omitted.
(3) Section 104 of that Act (general provisions as to appropriation and disposal of land).	Subsections (7) and (8) (power of Secretary of State to require local authority to dispose of land in certain cases and to resolve differences as to the best consideration in those cases) shall be omitted.
(4) Section 105 of that Act (default powers of Secretary of State).	The section shall cease to have effect.

Enactment relating to local authority function	*Amendment*
7.—(1) Section 43 of the Diseases of Animals Act 1950 (power of local authority to provide facilities for sheepdipping).	The words "with the sanction of the Minister" shall be omitted.
(2) Section 61 of that Act (provision of wharves, etc.).	Subsection (7) (power of Minister to require a reduction in the tolls taken by a local authority) shall be omitted.
8. Section 1 of the Pet Animals Act 1951 (licensing of pet shops by local authorities).	In subsection (2), as originally enacted, the words "not exceeding ten shillings" shall be omitted.
9. Section 19 of the Mineral Workings Act 1951 (disposal of land acquired by local authorities).	In subsection (2) (power of Secretary of State to require a local authority to dispose of land acquired for certain purposes) the words from "but the local authority" to the end of the subsection shall be omitted.
10. Section 6 of the Pests Act 1954 (Order in Council may authorise a port health authority to make and recover charges for inspection of ships and hovercraft).	The words from the beginning to "may authorise" shall be omitted; for the words "to make and recover charges" there shall be substituted the words "may impose such charges as appear to the authority to be appropriate"; and for the words "any such Order in Council" there shall be substituted the words "any Order in Council under section 23 of the Prevention of Damage by Pests Act 1949".
11. Section 80 of the Food and Drugs Act 1955 (power of local authorities to provide cold stores and refrigerators).	In subsection (1) (power of a local authority, with the approval of the Minister, to provide a cold-air store or refrigerator for the storage and preservation of food) the words "with the approval of the Minister" shall be omitted. Subsection (3) (advertisement of local authority's intention to apply for Minister's approval) shall be omitted.
12. Section 124 of the Highways Act 1959 (power of highway authorities to require removal of structures from highway).	Subsection (2) (power of Secretary of State to extend time limit specified by highway authority for removal of structure) shall be omitted and in subsection (3) the words from "or, in a case where" to "so extended" and the words from "or, if an appeal" to the end of the subsection shall be omitted.
13. Schedule 2 to the Caravan Sites and Control of Development Act 1960 (orders of district councils prohibiting caravans on commons).	In paragraph 3, sub-paragraph (1) (service of notices and power of Secretary of State to dispense with service) for the words "Provided that where" there shall be substituted the words "unless the council are satisfied that" and the words from "the Minister" to the end of the sub-paragraph shall be omitted.

Enactment relating to local authority function	*Amendment*
14. Section 2 of the Local Authorities (Land) Act 1963 (power of local authorities to develop land for the benefit or improvement of their area).	Subsections (2) and (3) (consent of Secretary of State required for local authorities to develop land) shall be omitted.
15.—(1) Section 4 (2) of the Weights and Measures Act 1963 (local standards to be kept and used at approved premises).	After the word "kept" there shall be inserted the words "in such manner and under such conditions as the Secretary of State may direct", the words "and approved for the purpose by the Board" shall be omitted and for the words "approved in that behalf by the Board" there shall be substituted the words "which appear to the authority to be appropriate".
(2) Section 5 (3) of that Act (working standards and testing and stamping equipment to be kept at approved premises).	The words "and approved for the purpose by the Board" shall be omitted.
(3) Section 44 (1) of that Act (no discount to be given in respect of inspectors' fees except with consent).	The words "with the consent of the Board" shall be omitted.
16. Schedule 12 to the London Government Act 1963 (licensing of public entertainments in Greater London).	In each of paragraphs 3 and 6 (fees payable on application for licences for differing types of public entertainments to be such as the Greater London Council may fix, within specified limits) the words from "not exceeding" to the end of the paragraph shall be omitted.
17. Section 1 of the Animal Boarding Establishments Act 1963 (licensing by local authorities of boarding establishments for animals).	In subsection (2), as originally enacted, the words "not exceeding ten shillings" shall be omitted.
18. Section 1 of the Riding Establishments Act 1964 (licensing of riding establishments by local authorities).	In subsection (2), for the words from "and on payment" to "grant" there shall be substituted the words "grant, on payment of such fee as may be determined by the local authority".
19.—(1) Section 5 of the Plant Health Act 1967 (execution of Act by local authorities).	In subsection (2) (local authorities to keep certain records in such manner and form as competent authority may direct), the words from "in such manner" to "direct" shall be omitted.
(2) Section 6 of that Act (publication of orders).	In subsection (3) (local authorities to publish orders in such manner and form as competent authority directs) the words from "in such manner as the competent authority directs" to "such direction" shall be omitted.
20.—(1) Section 12 of the Road Traffic Regulation Act 1967 (temporary prohibition or restriction of traffic on roads).	In subsection (6) (order made by highway authority, other than a Minister, restricting or prohibiting use of road not to continue in force for a longer period than six weeks from the making

Enactment relating to local authority function	*Amendment*
20. The Road Traffic Regulation Act 1967—*cont.*	thereof without the Secretary of State's approval) after the words "by a Minister" there shall be inserted the words "or the Greater London Council", for the words "six weeks" there shall be substituted the words "three months", for the word "making" there shall be substituted the words "coming into operation", and at the end of the subsection there shall be added the words "The reference in this subsection to an order made by the Greater London Council does not include a reference to an order made by any other body, in the exercise of delegated powers, as agents for the Greater London Council".
(2) Section 29 of that Act (additional powers of local authorities in connection with off-street parking places).	In subsection (1) (additional powers exercisable with Secretary of State's approval) the words from "exercisable" to "approved by him" shall be omitted.
(3) Section 31 of that Act (power of local authorities by order to make provision as to use of parking places).	In subsection (2) (where order provides for use of apparatus for collecting charges, local authorities to comply with Secretary of State's directions as to testing, etc. thereof) the words from "and, where an order provides for the use of any apparatus" to the end of the subsection shall be omitted.
(4) Section 37 (5) of that Act (local authority to take prescribed steps for inspection and testing on prescribed occasions of parking meters and for recording in prescribed manner the date on which and the person by whom a meter has been tested).	For the words "the prescribed steps" there shall be substituted the words "such steps as appear to them to be appropriate", for the words from "not less" to "occasions" there shall be substituted the word "afterwards", and the words "in the prescribed manner" and the words from "and in this" onwards shall be omitted.
(5) Section 44 of that Act (financial provisions relating to parking places).	In the proviso to subsection (2) (local authority's surplus not to be carried forward from one quadrennial period to another without Secretary of State's consent) the words from "but shall not be carried forward" onwards shall be omitted and in subsection (3) (*c*) (surplus may be applied in making contributions towards cost of parking accommodation provided by other local authorities or, with Secretary of State's consent, by other persons) the words "with the consent of the appropriate Minister" shall be omitted.

Enactment relating to local authority function	*Amendment*
20. The Road Traffic Regulation Act 1967—*cont.*	
(6) Section 46 of that Act (power of parish and community councils to provide parking places).	In subsection (2) (power of councils to appropriate land, with Secretary of State's consent, for the purpose of providing parking places) the words "with the consent of the Minister of Housing and Local Government" shall be omitted.
21.—(1) Section 12 of the Health Services and Public Health Act 1968 (power of certain local authorities to make arrangements for prophylaxis, care and after-care).	In subsection (5) (power of authorities, with Secretary of State's approval, to recover charges for services) the words "with the approval of the Minister" shall be omitted.
(2) Section 13 of that Act (provision by certain local authorities of home help and laundry facilities).	In subsection (2) (power of authorities, with Secretary of State's approval, to recover charges for help or facilities provided) the words "with the approval of the Minister" shall be omitted.
22.—(1) Section 10 of the Transport Act 1968 (general powers of Passenger Transport Executive).	In subsection (1) (xvi) (power, with Passenger Transport Authority's approval and Secretary of State's consent, to make arrangements for transfer of part of Executive's undertaking or property to persons who have agreed to carry on any of Executive's activities) the words "and the consent of the Minister" shall be omitted.
(2) Section 11 of that Act (financial duty of Executive).	Subsection (4) (Executive to submit to Secretary of State statement of Executive's proposals for expenditure on capital account and power of Secretary of State to limit such expenditure) shall be omitted.
(3) Section 12 of that Act (borrowing powers of Executive).	In subsection (4) (power of certain councils to lend money to Executive and, with Secretary of State's consent, to borrow money for that purpose) the words "with the consent of the Minister" shall be omitted.
(4) Section 13 of that Act (power for Authority to precept for Executive).	Subsection (4) (power of Secretary of State to restrict the aggregate amount for which Authority may issue precepts) shall be omitted.
(5) Section 16 of that Act (publication of annual report by Authority and Executive and prevention of improper conduct of subsidiary activities).	In subsection (2), in paragraph (*c*), the final word "and" and paragraph (*d*) (in certain cases report to contain such information as the Secretary of State may direct) shall be omitted, and subsections (3) to (5) (Secretary of State's powers to control conduct of certain types of business carried on by an Executive and subsidiaries thereof) shall be omitted.

Enactment relating to local authority function	*Amendment*
22. The Transport Act 1968—*cont.*	
(6) Section 18 of that Act (planning of passenger transport services in designated areas).	In subsection (1) (statement of general policy to be prepared within twelve months of establishment of Authority, or such longer period as the Secretary of State allows, and copies to be sent to the Secretary of State and to local authorities concerned) the words "to the Minister and" shall be omitted, and in subsection (2) (plan for development of passenger transport system to be prepared within two years of establishment of Executive, or such longer period as the Secretary of State allows, and copies to be sent to the Secretary of State and to local authorities concerned) the words "to the Minister and" shall be omitted.
(7) Section 19 of that Act (transfer of control of bus services to Executive).	In subsection (1) (power of Secretary of State, after receiving copy of statement prepared under section 18 (1), to transfer control of bus services to Executive) for the words from "Minister has received" to "a copy of" there shall be substituted the words "Authority for a designated area have caused to be published".
(8) Section 21 of that Act (provisions as to functions of traffic commissioners in connection with designated areas).	In subsection (5), paragraph (*a*) (regulations of Secretary of State may require Executive to furnish commissioners with information as to certain road passenger transport services) shall be omitted.
(9) Section 36 of that Act (power of local authority to run public service vehicles as contract carriages).	In subsection (2), the words "subject to subsection (3) of this section" and subsections (3) to (8) (control by Secretary of State over exercise of local authorities' powers) shall be omitted.
(10) Section 37 of that Act (power of local authorities, with the Secretary of State's consent, to acquire or dispose of public service vehicle undertakings).	In subsection (1), the words from "with the consent" to "Secretary of State" and subsection (2) (terms on which consent may be given) shall be omitted.
(11) Section 138 of that Act (power of a local authority to make arrangements to reimburse, and to contribute towards, costs incurred by other bodies in granting travel concessions).	Subsections (7) and (8) (power of Secretary of State to prescribe method of calculating cost incurred in providing travel concessions and to make regulations about determinations of disputes with respect to such cost) shall be omitted.
(12) Part III of Schedule 5 to that Act (matters which may be dealt with by an order designating a passenger transport area).	Paragraph 14 (making of reports and furnishing of information by Authority and Executive to Secretary of State) shall be omitted.

Enactment relating to local authority function	*Amendment*
23.—(1) Section 7 of the Transport (London) Act 1969 (financial duty of London Transport Executive).	Subsection (5) (Executive to submit to Secretary of State statement of Executive's proposals for expenditure on capital account and power of Secretary of State to limit such expenditure) shall be omitted.
(2) Section 12 of that Act (Secretary of State's power to prevent improper conduct of subsidiary activities).	In subsection (2), in paragraph (*c*), the final word "and" and paragraph (*d*) (in certain cases, annual report of Executive to contain such information as the Secretary of State may direct) shall be omitted, and subsections (3) to (5) (Secretary of State's powers to control conduct of certain types of business carried on by Executive and subsidiaries thereof) shall be omitted.
24.—(1) Section 3 of the Late Night Refreshment Houses Act 1969 (annual duty payable to licensing authority in respect of licence to keep late night refreshment house).	In subsection (1) (duty of £6 payable in respect of licence), for the words from "charged" to "to the licensing authority" there shall be substituted the words "payable to the licensing authority a fee of such amount as appears to them to be appropriate" and for the word "duty", in the second place where it occurs, there shall be substituted the word "fee", and subsections (2) and (3) (power of Secretary of State by order to vary or dispense with licence duty) shall be omitted.
(2) Sections 4 and 5 of that Act (reduced duty on beginner's part-year licence and date of licence and period of validity).	For the word "duty", in each place where it occurs, there shall be substituted the word "fee" and for the word "chargeable" (in section 5 (2)) there shall be substituted the word "payable".
25.—(1) Section 28 of the Town and Country Planning Act 1971 (publicity for applications for planning permission for development affecting conservation areas).	In subsection (1) (types of development with which section is concerned) the word "either", paragraph (*b*) and the word "or" immediately preceding it shall be omitted.
(2) Section 31 of that Act (directions etc. to local planning authorities as to method of dealing with applications).	Subsections (2) and (3) (directions with respect to applications affecting conservation areas) shall be omitted.
(3) Section 46 of that Act (procedure where revocation or modification of planning permission by local planning authority is unopposed).	In subsection (1), paragraph (*b*) (procedure conditional on it appearing to the authority that no claim for compensation is likely to arise under section 164) and the word "and" immediately preceding it shall be omitted and in subsection (3) (service of notice, and notice to include a statement that no compensation is payable) the words from "and the notice" to the end of the subsection shall be omitted.

Enactment relating to local authority function	*Amendment*
25. The Town and Country Planning Act 1971—*cont.*	
(4) Section 65 of that Act (power of local planning authority, subject to Secretary of State's directions, to serve notice requiring proper maintenance of waste land).	In subsection (1), the words "then, subject to any directions given by the Secretary of State" shall be omitted.
(5) Section 87 (1) of that Act (power of local planning authority, subject to Secretary of State's directions, to serve enforcement notice).	The words "any directions given by the Secretary of State and to" shall be omitted.
(6) Section 96 (1) of that Act (power of local planning authority, subject to Secretary of State's directions, to serve listed building enforcement notice).	The words "then, subject to any directions given by the Secretary of State" shall be omitted.
(7) Section 100 (1) of that Act (power of Secretary of State to give directions to local planning authorities requiring them to serve listed building enforcement notices or to serve such notices himself).	The words from "give directions" to "or may" shall be omitted.
(8) Section 117 of that Act (direction for minimum compensation in case of listed building deliberately left derelict).	In subsection (1) (power of authority to include in compulsory purchase order as submitted to Secretary of State for confirmation an application for a direction for minimum compensation) the words "an application for" and the words from "and the Secretary of State" to the end of the subsection shall be omitted, in subsection (3) (notice stating effect of compulsory purchase order to include statement that authority have made application for direction for minimum compensation) for the words "made application for" there shall be substituted the words "included in the order" and in subsection (5) (power to object to directions for minimum compensation) the words "an application for", "the local authority's application for" and "be refused or, as the case may be, that such a direction" shall be omitted and after the words "order as" there shall be inserted the words "confirmed or".
(9) Section 124 of that Act (power of local authority to develop land held for planning purposes).	Subsections (3) and (4) (Secretary of State's consent requisite to any exercise of authority's power) shall be omitted, in subsection (6) (power of authority, with Secretary of State's consent, to enter into arrangements with authorised association for the carrying out by the association of development)

Enactment relating to local authority function	*Amendment*
25. The Town and Country Planning Act 1971—*cont.*	the words "with the consent of the Secretary of State" shall be omitted and in subsection (8) (authorised associations defined as certain societies, companies or bodies of persons approved by the Secretary of State) the words "approved by the Secretary of State" shall be omitted.
(10) Section 125 of that Act (special provisions as to features and buildings of architectural and historic interest).	In subsection (1) (local authority, in exercising certain powers, to have regard to the desirability of preserving features of special architectural or historic interest and Secretary of State, in giving consent under certain provisions, to ensure the preservation of listed buildings) the words from "and the Secretary of State" to the end of the subsection shall be omitted and, consequentially, subsection (2) and in subsection (3) the words from " "preservation", in" to "and" shall be omitted.
(11) Section 164 (1) of that Act (where planning permission is revoked or modified by an order, other than an order taking effect by virtue of section 46 and without being confirmed by the Secretary of State, the local planning authority is to pay compensation).	The words from "(other than" to "Secretary of State)" shall be omitted.
(12) Section 276 of that Act (default powers of Secretary of State).	In subsection (1) (power of Secretary of State to give directions to local planning authorities requiring them to submit to him certain orders for his confirmation or to make such orders himself) the words from "give directions" to "or may" shall be omitted and in subsection (5) (power of Secretary of State to give directions to local planning authorities requiring them to serve certain notices or to serve such notices himself) paragraph (*b*), in paragraph (*c*) the words from "or under" to "this Act" and the words from "give directions" to "or may" shall be omitted.
(13) Section 277 of that Act (designation of conservation areas).	Subsection (2) (power of Secretary of State to give directions to local planning authorities with respect to designation of conservation areas) shall be omitted.
(14) Schedule 11 to that Act (control of works for demolition, alteration or extension of listed buildings).	In paragraph 11, in sub-paragraph (1) (power of Secretary of State to give directions to a local planning authority

Enactment relating to local authority function	*Amendment*
25. The Town and Country Planning Act 1971—*cont.*	requiring them to submit to him for his confirmation an order revoking or modifying listed building consent in respect of certain works or to make such an order himself) the words from "give directions" to "or may" shall be omitted.
26.—(1) Section 18 of the Slaughter-houses Act 1974 (power to provide cold stores and refrigerators for public slaughterhouses).	In subsection (1) (power of a local authority with the approval of the Minister, to provide cold store or refrigerator for the storage and preservation of meat and other articles of food) the words "with the approval of the Minister" shall be omitted and subsections (3) to (5) (advertisement of local authority's intention to apply for Minister's approval and provisions as to public inquiries) shall be omitted.
(2) Section 40 (9) of that Act (power of local authority to charge fixed fees for grant and renewal of licence).	For the words from "a fee", in the first place where they occur, to "5p" there shall be substituted the words "such fees as appear to them to be appropriate for the grant and". **[258]**

SCHEDULE 7

Section 42

Minor and Consequential Amendments

The National Parks and Access to the Countryside Act 1949

1. In paragraph (*e*) of section 97 (1) of the National Parks and Access to the Countryside Act 1949 for the words from "any of" to the end of the paragraph there shall be substituted the words "section 89 (5) or section 103 (5) of this Act for the purpose of their functions under section 89 (2) of this Act". **[259]**

The Local Government Act 1966

2.—(1) In section 27 of the Local Government Act 1966, in subsection (3), after the words "this Act" there shall be inserted the words "(in this section referred to as an 'existing enactment or instrument')" and for the words from "is classified" to the end of the subsection there shall be substituted the following paragraphs—

"(*a*) is classified under subsection (2) of this section, or continues to be treated under section 40 of the Local Government Act 1974, as a principal road for the purposes of any enactment or instrument which refers to roads or highways classified by the Secretary of State as principal roads; or

(*b*) is classified under subsection (2) of this section as a classified road for the purposes of that existing enactment or instrument."

(2) In subsection (4) of that section, for the words from "every such" to the end of the subsection there shall be substituted the words "every existing enactment or instrument". **[260]**

The General Rate Act 1967

3. In section 12 (9) of the General Rate Act 1967 (interest on amounts due under precepts which are not paid on or before the date specified for payment) after the words "six per cent. per annum" there shall be inserted the words "or such other rate as may be either prescribed or determined in a prescribed manner".

4.—(1) In section 48 of that Act, in subsection (1) (*a*), for the words "in pursuance of paragraph 1 of Part III of Schedule 1 to the Local Government Act 1966" there shall be substituted the words "for their area under paragraph 5 of Schedule 2 to the Local Government Act 1974".

(2) In subsection (4) of that section for the words "Part III of Schedule 1 to the said Act of 1966" there shall be substituted the words "paragraph 5 of Schedule 2 to the Local Government Act 1974".

5. In section 51 (1) of that Act (power of rating authority to grant discount not exceeding $2\frac{1}{2}$ per cent. in respect of rates on dwelling-houses) the words "not exceeding two-and-a-half per cent." shall be omitted.

6. Section 52 of that Act shall cease to have effect.

7. In section 54 (1) of that Act (power of rating authority to make allowance by way of discount not exceeding $2\frac{1}{2}$ per cent. in respect of rates on all hereditaments) for the words "not exceeding two and a half per cent." there shall be substituted the words "of such amount as may be specified in the resolution".

8. In paragraph (*a*) of subsection (1) of section 113 of that Act (power to make rules prescribing certain matters and the form of certain documents) after the words "the form of" there shall be inserted the words "or the matters to be specified in".

9. In section 115 (3) of that Act for the words "sections 49 and 50" there shall be substituted the words "section 50", in paragraph (*a*) for the words from "relevant date" to the end of sub-paragraph (ii) there shall be substituted the words "date of the giving of a notice under subsection (1) of that section", paragraph (*b*) shall be omitted and for paragraph (*c*) there shall be substituted the following paragraph—

"(*c*) if at the date of the giving of a notice under the said subsection (1) a rebate is for the time being payable in respect of the hereditament or any part thereof under the statutory rate rebate scheme, within the meaning of Part II of the Local Government Act 1974 or, as the case may be, a local rate rebate scheme, within the meaning of that Part".

10. Schedule 11 to that Act shall cease to have effect. [**261**]

The Local Government Act 1972

11. In section 81 of the Local Government Act 1972 (exceptions to provisions about disqualification in section 80) after subsection (3) there shall be inserted the following subsection:—

"(3A) Section 80 (1) (*a*) above shall not operate to disqualify any person for being elected or being the chairman, vice-chairman, deputy chairman or an alderman or councillor of the Greater London Council by reason of his being employed by the London Transport Executive or any subsidiary of theirs"

12. In paragraph 7 of Schedule 13 to that Act, in sub-paragraph (1), after the words "subject to" there shall be inserted the words "sub-paragraph (3) and" and at the end of that paragraph there shall be added the following sub-paragraph:—

"(3) In any case where—

(*a*) a local authority make an advance to any other person (including another authority) and the expenditure incurred in making the advance is defrayed by borrowing, and
(*b*) the terms of that advance are such that repayment is to be made otherwise than by equal instalments of principal and interest combined, and

(*c*) apart from this sub-paragraph, the local authority would have no power, with respect to the expenditure referred to in paragraph (*a*) above, to vary the sums which would otherwise be debited under sub-paragraph (1) above or to suspend their obligation under that sub-paragraph,

the local authority may, under sub-paragraph (1) above, debit the account from which the expenditure referred to in paragraph (*a*) above would otherwise fall to be defrayed with sums of different amounts (whether or not including instalments of principal) in respect of different years in order to take account of the terms on which their advance falls to be repaid." **[262]**

The Water Act 1973

13.—(1) In paragraph 11 (9) of Schedule 5 to the Water Act 1973 the words from "multiplied by" to "authority for that year" shall be omitted.

(2) In paragraph 11 (13) of that Schedule, for the definition of "the appropriate factor" there shall be substituted the words " 'actual penny rate product', in relation to any area, means the product of a rate of 1p in the pound for that area as determined for the purposes of this paragraph in accordance with rules made under section 113 (1) (*c*) of the General Rate Act 1967" and the definition of "the conclusive calculation" shall be omitted.

(3) In paragraph 13 (1) of that Schedule for the words "in accordance with this paragraph" there shall be substituted the words "as mentioned in sub-paragraph (3) below".

(4) Paragraph 13 (2) of that Schedule shall be omitted.

(5) In sub-paragraph (3) of paragraph 13 of that Schedule for the words from "as estimated" to the end of the sub-paragraph there shall be substituted the words "as determined for the purposes of this Part of this Schedule in accordance with rules made under section 113 (1) (*c*) of the General Rate Act 1967, and the appropriate penny rate product as so determined for any area for the relevant year and any information relevant to that determination which may be specified in those rules shall be notified to the water authority at such time and in such manner as may be so specified".

14. In Schedule 6 to that Act, in paragraph 5 (2), in paragraph (*c*) after the words "transitional period" there shall be inserted the words "in respect of which no provision is made by an agreement uuder section 32A of this Act" and at the end of the said paragraph (*c*) there shall be inserted the following paragraph:—

"(*cc*) without prejudice to the generality of paragraph (*c*) above, for the demand, collection and recovery by a local authority of any such amount as is mentioned in that paragraph in like manner as, and together with, any amount due to the authority in respect of the general rate and for the extension of section 113 of, and the modification of Schedule 12 to, the General Rate Act 1967 (power to make rules, and forms of documents) to take account of any such provision made by the order.". **[263]**

The Breeding of Dogs Act 1973

15.—(1) Section 4 of the Breeding of Dogs Act 1973 (which confers power on a local authority to prosecute for certain offences but is rendered unnecessary by section 111 of the Local Government Act 1972) shall cease to have effect.

(2) In section 5 (2) of that Act, in the definition of local authority, after the word "means" there shall be inserted the words "in England and Wales" and for the words from "or of a district" to "Wales)" there shall be substituted the words "the council of a district". **[264]**

NOTE

For ministerial explanation of para. 12, see H. of C. Official Report, S.C.A., 14th December 1973.

SCHEDULE 8

Section 42

ENACTMENTS REPEALED

Chapter	Short Title	Extent of Repeal
15 & 16 Geo. 5 c. 38	The Performing Animals (Regulation) Act 1925	In section 1, in subsection (5) the words "on payment of the prescribed fee", in both places where they occur, and in subsection (7) the words "subject to payment of the prescribed fee". In section 5, in subsection (3) the words from "and the fee for registration" to the end of the subsection.
26 Geo. 5 & 1 Edw. 8 c. 49	The Public Health Act 1936	Section 292.
10 & 11 Geo. 6 c. 22	The Civic Restaurants Act 1947	In section 3, in subsection (1) the words from "and the form of the account" to the end of the subsection, and in subsection (2) the words from "and if the account" to the end of the subsection.
11 & 12 Geo. 6 c. 26	The Local Government Act 1948	Section 138 (2).
12, 13 & 14 Geo. 6 c. 55	The Prevention of Damage by Pests Act 1949	In section 7 (2) the words "two hundred and ninety-two" and the words "for the inclusion of sums in respect of establishment charges in expenses recoverable under that Act".
12, 13 & 14 Geo. 6 c. 97	The National Parks and Access to the Countryside Act 1949	In section 64 (1) the words "with the approval of the Minister". Section 65 (6). In section 97, in subsection (1), paragraphs (*a*) and (*b*), and in paragraph (*c*) the words from "and under" to the end of the paragraph, and subsections (6) and (7). Section 98. In section 104, subsections (7) and (8). Section 105.
14 Geo. 6 c. 36	The Diseases of Animals Act 1950	In section 43 the words "with the sanction of the Minister". Section 61 (7).
14 & 15 Geo. 6 c. 35	The Pet Animals Act 1951	In section 1 (2), as originally enacted, the words "not exceeding ten shillings".
14 & 15 Geo. 6 c. 60	The Mineral Workings Act 1951	In section 19, in subsection (2) the words from "but the local authority" to the end of the subsection, and subsection (4).

Chapter	Short Title	Extent of Repeal
2 & 3 Eliz. 2 c. 68	The Pests Act 1954	In section 6 the words from the beginning to "may authorise".
4 & 5 Eliz. 2 c. 16	The Food and Drugs Act 1955	In section 80, in subsection (1), the words "with the approval of the Minister", and subsection (3).
7 & 8 Eliz. 2 c. 25	The Highways Act 1959	In section 124, subsection (2), and in subsection (3) the words from "or, in a case where" to "so extended" and the words from "or, if an appeal" to the end of the subsection. In section 174 (2) (*b*) the words from "which may include" to "and notices".
8 & 9 Eliz. 2 c. 62	The Caravan Sites and Control of Development Act 1960	In Schedule 2, in paragraph 3, in sub-paragraph (1) the words from "the Minister" to the end of the sub-paragraph.
1963 c. 29	The Local Authorities (Land) Act 1963	In section 2, subsections (2) and (3).
1963 c. 31	The Weights and Measures Act 1963	In section 4 (2) the words "and approved for the purpose by the Board". In section 5 (3) the words "and approved for the purpose by the Board". In section 44 (1) the words "with the consent of the Board".
1963 c. 33	The London Government Act 1963	In Schedule 12, in each of paragraphs 3 and 6, the words from "not exceeding" to the end of the paragraph.
1963 c. 43	The Animal Boarding Establishments Act 1963	In section 1 (2), as originally enacted, the words "not exceeding ten shillings".
1966 c. 9	The Rating Act 1966	Section 9. Section 12 (*a*).
1966 c. 42	The Local Government Act 1966	Sections 1 to 5. Section 8. Section 10. In section 27 (2) the words from "all or any" to "authorities, and". Schedule 1. In Schedule 3, in Part II, in column 1 the entries numbered 11, 14, 16, 21, 24, 25, 26 and 28.
1967 c. 8	The Plant Health Act 1967	In section 5 (2) the words from "in such manner" to "direct".

Chapter	Short Title	Extent of Repeal
1967 c. 8—*cont.*	The Plant Health Act 1967 —*cont.*	In section 6 (3) the words from "in such manner as the competent authority directs" to "such direction".
1967 c. 9	The General Rate Act 1967	In section 17 (2), in paragraph (*a*) the words from "not being earlier" to the end of the paragraph, and in paragraph (*b*) the words from "not being earlier" to the end of the paragraph. In section 21 (7) the words "or in section 22 of this Act". Section 22. Section 35. Section 49. In section 51 (1) the words "not exceeding two-and-a-half per cent". Section 52. In section 115, in subsection (1) the definitions of "rebate application" and "rebate period", and subsection (3) (*b*). Schedules 9 and 11.
1967 c. 76	The Road Traffic Regulation Act 1967	In section 29, in subsection (1) the words from "exercisable" to "approved by him", and subsection (2). In section 31, in subsection (2) the words from "and, where an order provides" to the end of the subsection. In section 37, in subsection (5) the words "in the prescribed manner" and the words from "and in this" onwards. In section 44, in subsection (2), in the proviso the words from "but shall not be carried forward" to the end of the proviso, and in subsection (3) (*c*) the words "with the consent of the appropriate Minister". In section 46 (2) the words "with the consent of the Minister of Housing and Local Government". In section 72 (6) (*a*) the words "for the purposes of advances under section 235 of the Highways Act 1959". In section 84B (8) (*a*) the words "for the purposes of advances under section 235 of the Highways Act 1959".

Chapter	Short Title	Extent of Repeal
1968 c. 41	The Countryside Act 1968	In section 2 (9) the words "this Act or". Section 5. Sections 33 to 35. In section 36, in subsection (1) the words from "under this Act" to "making of grants", and in subsection (8) the words from "and subsections (2)" onwards.
1968 c. 46	The Health Services and Public Health Act 1968	In section 12 (5) the words "with the approval of the Minister". In section 13 (2), the words "with the approval of the Minister".
1968 c. 73	The Transport Act 1968	In section 10 (1) (xvi) the words "and the consent of the Minister". In section 11, subsections (4) and (5). In section 12 (4) the words "with the consent of the Minister". In section 13, subsections (4) and (7). In section 15, in subsection (4) the words from "to the provisions" to the end of the subsection. In section 16, in subsection (2), in paragraph (*c*) the final word "and" and paragraph (*d*), and subsections (3) to (5). In section 18, in each of subsections (1) and (2), the words "to the Minister and". Section 21 (5) (*a*). In section 34, subsections (2) and (3). In section 36, in subsection (2) the words "subject to subsection (3) of this section", and subsections (3) to (8). In section 37, in subsection (1) the words from "with the consent" to "Secretary of State", and subsection (2). In section 138, subsections (6) to (8) and (9) (*a*). In Schedule 5, in Part III paragraph 14. In Schedule 14, in Part IV paragraph 10.
1969 c. 10	The Mines and Quarries (Tips) Act 1969	In section 23 (1), paragraph (*c*) except the final word "and".

Chapter	Short Title	Extent of Repeal
1969 c. 33	The Housing Act 1969	Section 74.
1969 c. 35	The Transport (London) Act 1969	In section 3, in subsection (1) the words from "but any expenditure" to the end of the subsection. In section 7, subsection (5) and in subsection (6), in paragraph (*a*) the final word "and" and paragraphs (*b*) and (*c*). In section 12, in subsection (2), in paragraph (*c*) the final word "and" and paragraph (*d*), and subsections (3) to (5). In section 23 (6), paragraph (*b*) and the word "and" immediately preceding it. In section 29 (1) (*a*) the words "for the purposes of advances under section 235 of the Highways Act 1959".
1969 c. 53	The Late Night Refreshment Houses Act 1969	In section 3, subsections (2) and (3). Section 12.
1970 c. 21	The New Forest Act 1970	Section 4.
1970 c. 32	The Riding Establishments Act 1970	In section 2 (1), paragraph (i).
1971 c. 41	The Highways Act 1971	In section 1 (6) (*a*) (i) the words "for the purposes of advances under section 235 of the principal Act".
1971 c. 78	The Town and Country Planning Act 1971	In section 28 (1) the word "either", paragraph (*b*) and the word "or" immediately preceding it. In section 31, subsections (2) and (3). In section 46, in subsection (1) paragraph (*b*) and the word "and" immediately preceding it, and in subsection (3) the words from "and the notice" to the end of the subsection. In section 65 (1) the words "then, subject to any directions given by the Secretary of State". In section 87 (1) the words "any directions given by the Secretary of State and to". In section 91 (4), paragraph (*c*) except the final word "and". In section 96 (1) the words "then, subject to any directions given by the Secretary of State".

Chapter	Short Title	Extent of Repeal
1971 c. 78—*cont.*	The Town and Country Planning Act 1971—*cont.*	In section 100 (1) the words from "give directions" to "or may". In section 117, in subsection (1) the words "an application for" and the words from "and the Secretary of State" to the end of the subsection, and in subsection (5) the words "an application for", "the local authority's application for" and "be refused or, as the case may be, that such a direction". In section 124, subsections (3) and (4), in subsection (6) the words "with the consent of the Secretary of State" and in subsection (8) the words "approved by the Secretary of State". In section 125, in subsection (1) the words from "and the Secretary of State" to the end of the subsection, subsection (2) and in subsection (3) the words from " "preservation", in" to "and". In section 164 (1) the words from "(other than" to "Secretary of State)". In section 212 (1) the words "for the purposes of advances under section 235 of the Highways Act 1959". In section 276, in subsection (1) the words from "give directions" to "or may" and in subsection (5) paragraph (*b*), in paragraph (*c*) the words from "or under" to "this Act" and the words from "give directions" to "or may". Section 277 (2). In Schedule 11, in paragraph 11 (1) the words from "give directions" to "or may".
1971 c. lxx	The Chichester Harbour Conservancy Act 1971	Section 30 (3).
1972 c. 47	The Housing Finance Act 1972	In Schedule 9, paragraphs 7 and 8.
1972 c. 70	The Local Government Act 1972	Section 203 (5). In Schedule 24, paragraph 11, and in paragraph 12, in section 13 of the Transport Act 1968 as set out in that paragraph, subsection (2).
1973 c. 28	The Rate Rebate Act 1973	The whole Act.

Chapter	Short Title	Extent of Repeal
1973 c. 37	The Water Act 1973	In Schedule 5, in paragraph 11 (9) the words from "multiplied by" to "authority for that year", in paragraph 11 (13) the definition of "the conclusive calculation" and paragraph 13 (2).
1973 c. 60	The Breeding of Dogs Act 1973	Section 4.
1974 c. 3	The Slaughterhouses Act 1974	In section 18, in subsection (1) the words "with the approval of the Minister" and subsections (3) to (5). In Schedule 3, paragraphs 3 and 6.

[265]

INDEX

All references are to paragraph numbers

All references are to paragraph numbers

All references are to paragraph numbers

All references are to paragraph numbers

All references are to paragraph numbers

All references are to paragraph numbers

Index

All references are to paragraph numbers

All references are to paragraph numbers

All references are to paragraph numbers